Douglas Levi

SURVIVING THE INSURANCE JUNGLE

How to get the best value for where 11% of your budget goes

outskirts press

Surviving the Insurance Jungle
How to get the best value for where 11% of your budget goes
All Rights Reserved.
Copyright © 2017 Douglas Levi
v1.0 r1.0

The opinions expressed in this manuscript are solely the opinions of the author and do not represent the opinions or thoughts of the publisher. The author has represented and warranted full ownership and/or legal right to publish all the materials in this book.

This book may not be reproduced, transmitted, or stored in whole or in part by any means, including graphic, electronic, or mechanical without the express written consent of the publisher except in the case of brief quotations embodied in critical articles and reviews.

Outskirts Press, Inc.
http://www.outskirtspress.com

ISBN: 978-1-4787-8132-5

Cover Photo © 2017 Shuttershock. All rights reserved - used with permission.

Outskirts Press and the "OP" logo are trademarks belonging to Outskirts Press, Inc.

PRINTED IN THE UNITED STATES OF AMERICA

Acknowledgements and Thanks:

To my Amy bear, my wife, and mother of our children I love you and adore you. Thank you for being my best friend and always being there for me. To our team at Strategic Insurance Services, keep taking superior care of our clients putting their needs above ours.

To my parents, Ned and Rosemary, I will never forget all the love and support you have given me over the years. Most importantly, to our Great God in heaven, I thank Him every day for the grace and mercy that Jesus Christ shows me.

Rave reviews for Surviving the Insurance Jungle:

"Surviving the Insurance Jungle is a common sense guide for one of the most important buying decisions a consumer can make. Obtaining the right insurance coverage can often be confusing. Doug debunks the myths and provides insurance buyers with sound advice."

Jeff Grady, CEO Florida Association of Insurance Agents

"Doug Levi doesn't simply know and understand the insurance marketplace. Doug is one the rare insurance professionals who owns the insurance expertise necessary to take his clients from survive to THRIVE!"

Ryan M Hanley, Managing Editor, Agencynation.com

"Surviving the Insurance Jungle is reminscent of the practical tips you would want to share with anyone starting out in life. If you are unsure about insurance, or how to get the best value for your dollar this is a must read."

Christopher Smoak, Financial Advisor, Prudential Financial

Table of Contents

Overview:
    Where 11% (or more) of your money goes i
Introduction v
Chapter 1:
    Brief Overview of Insurance - A Funny Story
    about Coffee and Boats 1
Chapter 2:
    Auto Insurance - Price vs. Cost 7
Chapter 3:
    Home Sweet Home - Protecting your house 17
Chapter 4:
    Health Insurance - How ACA has changed
    the landscape forever 26
Chapter 5:
    Disability Insurance - More than just a "Quack Quack" 34
Chapter 6:
    Life Insurance - A love letter to your family 43
Chapter 7:
    Flood Insurance - Splish, splash, I'm taking a bath 49
Chapter 8:
    Long-term CareInsurance - Age with the
    dignity you deserve 53
Chapter 9:
    Accident Insurance and what else DON'T I need? 58
Chapter 10:
    Umbrella Insurance - Protect against the big one 62
Summary:
    Pulling it altogether 65

Overview

Where 11% (or more) of your money goes

INSURANCE TOUCHES MOST areas of our lives. Like it or not, we live in a world ripe with challenges, and sometimes bad things happen. When it works well, insurance is there to help us recover and make us whole again. When it doesn't work, it can be frustrating beyond belief. Believe me—I've been there. The goal of this book is to break down the complex world of insurance into common-sense concepts you can use to protect your family, understand what you need (and what you don't need), and find the best coverage for the best price possible. **Insurance is something you never want until you absolutely need it. Then it's like water or oxygen and it is critically important.**

According to the Bureau of Labor Statistics, **the average American family spends almost 11% of their budget per YEAR on insurance! So for every $1000 the average US consumer spends, $110 goes to insurance.** That is a tremendous amount of the average American's budget when you think about it. While we all know insurance is necessary and important, let's be honest—no one likes paying for insurance. I know I don't and I own an insurance agency! That being said, I realize its importance and know the impact it has on real people. Most people want to pay for the minimum amount of coverage...**until they have a claim and then they want the maximum protection.** The focus of this book is to help make the purchasing of insurance as educated, informed, and wise as possible.

The chart below from the US Department of Labor shows what American expenditures were like from 2011 to 2013. Per below you can see **that approximately 10.8% of total spending was on insurance.**

US Bureau of Labor Statistics:[1]

Table A. Average annual expenditures and characteristics of all consumer units, 2011-2013

Item	2011	2012	2013
Average annual expenditures:			
Total	$49,705	$51,442	$51,100
Food	$6,458	$6,599	$6,602
At home	$3,838	$3,921	$3,977
Away from home	$2,620	$2,678	$2,625
Housing	$16,803	$16,887	$17,148
Apparel and services	$1,740	$1,736	$1,604
Transportation	$8,293	$8,998	$9,004
Healthcare	$3,313	$3,556	$3,631
Entertainment	$2,572	$2,605	$2,482
Cash contributions	$1,721	$1,913	$1,834
Personal insurance	$5,424	$5,591	$5,528
All other expenditures	$3,382	$3,557	$3,267

This book will give you the real world definitions we use each day to explain insurance in simple terms to our clients. Insurance is not rocket science, but it can certainly be complicated especially if you are not familiar in dealing with it. Like a lot of industries, insurance has its own "language," much of which I will break down in easy to understand concepts so you can feel confident as you structure a plan

[1] US Bureau of Statistics Expenditure Survey http://www.bls.gov/news.release/cesan.htm

for your family. This book is not meant to be a college course in insurance—**it is meant to be a survival guide that you and your busy family can use,** refer back to, and learn from to make good decisions with your hard-earned money.

In each chapter, we will give you:

- **3 Insurance Jungle Tips to understand,**
- **Practical ways to reduce your costs and increase your coverage,**
- **Real-life impact stories and examples from my career,**
- **Action steps for you to take, and**
- **Family protection points summary at end of each chapter**

Legal disclaimer: This book does not constitute legal or financial advice with regards to specific situations. Insurance is state specific, so as recommended numerous times in this book, it is always best to seek an advisor in your local area. This book does not offer guarantees for each client's situation but rather aims to educate and give a broad insurance overview. Remember, each client's situation can be different.

Introduction

INSURANCE HAS IMPACTED my life many times, and I'm sure it has impacted yours. My story of insurance starts with the fact that I shouldn't be here....at all. In 2007, I got hit by an SUV. I was crossing a busy street as a pedestrian and was hit by a Jeep that was flying at 65 miles per hour. SUVs win that battle versus pedestrians every time. When I was hit, I spun and was flung to the ground. When I realized I was still alive, disbelief set in. I spent the next week in the hospital recovering from a broken shoulder and shock to my system. Only by the grace of God am I still here and not paralyzed.

We've all heard the saying, "Life can change in an instant," and my brief story proves it. Think about my situation and all of the areas where insurance came into play: major medical health insurance for hospital bills, automobile liability insurance for the driver, disability insurance, if I had long term sustained injuries preventing me from working, and if I had died, life insurance and estate issues would have come in to play.

Getting hit by a Jeep in 2007 was certainly an unexpected challenge in my life, and the insurance I had helped tremendously for my medical bills. The goal of this book is to help educate YOU on how you can best protect your family by finding good coverage and maximizing discounts. **We'll share ways to reduce your insurance costs in some instances by 30%.**

At our agency, Strategic Insurance Services (SIS), we often talk with our team about our *"Why."* **Our *"Why"* is YOU! Yes, you reading**

this right now. See, we really believe in what we do, and we see firsthand the impact insurance has on people›s lives, **as it did for me years ago.** Our mission is, *"We help families and businesses Prepare, Protect and Recover from life's unexpected events. Move Forward. With Confidence.™"*

The driving force behind our company and what we do is taking care of the families and businesses that entrust Strategic Insurance with their hard earned money to protect themselves. It's what motivates us to strive for constantly adding value for our clients, and remembering that behind every insurance contract is a promise. That is our business, *"Protecting YOUR Why."*

Your "WHY" encompasses the most important people in your life hands down. Really that's the goal of insurance, to make sure that our most precious people are protected and also the assets we enjoy in our possession are safeguarded against something unforeseen happening. Your "WHY" is likely your husband, wife, son or daughter. **Things are replaceable, people are not.**

So we know the important people in our life constitute our most value "WHY's" and then we have our possessions. Let's be honest here. We are a society accustomed to having what we want, when we want it, including our possessions. Ever try to take a toy away from a toddler? How about an iPhone from a busy homemaker, or an Android smart phone away from businessman? We ALL have items we care about (probably too much) and at the top of the list is usually your home and cars, which along with life insurance, typically represent the foundation of a good family protection plan.

As you go through this book, **think about the true goal of insurance, to protect your "WHY's!"**

One last note here on this concept of possessions. In the winter of 2010 I went on my first mission trip with my church to Guatemala. It was a men's mission trip and we were building a small school for a very poor area of a village in Zacapa. I remember as we had meetings before we went to prepare for the trip, seeing pictures of these Guatemalan's and feeling pity for them for how poor they were. Well my first day there, we had a church service in what was a basic tin hut with only 3 walls. The joy and energy I saw from the native people was electrifying. It was also very humbling as I immediately felt convicted of my own arrogance thinking about how poor these people were months ago, in only monetary terms. In fact most of the Guatemalans there were some of the happiest people I have ever met with little more than probably the value of what you have in your shed or garage. So as you think about protecting your assets, remember that regardless of how much (or little) you have **your true value is never found in your possessions.**

My personal "WHY" below:

**Our kids (Fall 2018), from left to right:
Asher James Levi, Avery Gwen Levi, & Abigail Grace Levi.**

Having fun as a family at the beach! Honeymoon Island Beach, Sept 2018

My gorgeous & amazing wife Amy & myself:
Honeymoon Island Beach, Sept 2018

Online vs. Local in Person

Today so many people start their initial research online for just about anything (me included). Insurance happens to be an easy topic to look up and research. While that's good in many ways, for those people that choose to research, review and purchase directly online, what **they lose is the personal interaction of a Trusted Advisor**. I'm sure people reading this may have GEICO or ESurance or some other direct online insurance. I'm not here to slam these options at all. I'm here to make sure that **you are educated in your options.**

According to several recent studies the Millennial's (that is the younger generation with the most purchasing power now) although being tech savvy still prefer to purchase items, and services like insurance in person. Of course the research starts online, but they then prefer to wind up working with a real human being so they do not feel like they got 'ripped off.'[2]

Remember that insurance is a highly regulated industry and the rates are monitored and approved by the state. Agents get paid directly by the companies so any rate that an agent can offer you already includes the cost of their own commission. Therefore if you find a local advisor who has access to multiple companies and can help find you the best pricing for your insurance needs you would be best suited to go that route that online alone. When you do go online on your own you lack having someone to give ongoing advice, who knows your family and your changing needs. Calling and talking to an 800 # or placing a change online often leaves you without the counsel and advice you deserve to properly protect your "WHY's." In addition, online, is NOT always less expensive much to the surprise of many out there. Think GEICO is saving money by not having to pay agent's commissions? Well think about this, GEICO spends over $1,000,000,000 (that's 1 billion) annually on marketing alone. That lizard is everywhere and it certainly isn't free!

Jungle Tip #1- Find a good Trusted Choice Independent Agent who is committed to pro-active Protection Reviews. This is probably the single most important thing you can do to lower costs, improve coverage, and develop a solid protection plan that won't break the bank for your family.

At our agency, we are committed to periodic ongoing protection reviews with our clients to make sure they have the proper coverage for their family or business. We do this while reviewing the insurance market place to make sure our clients are getting the best possible rate. People are often surprised when they hear that we will review and existing client's coverage, and premium and recommend a switch to a less expensive, comparable policy (if appropriate). The reason is simple; at our agency we look to build lifelong relationships with our clients, and it is not only the right thing to do for the client, its more

---

[2] Engagex study- Millennial's Buy Insurance in Person http://blog.engagex.com/millennials-want-to-buy-insurance-in-person

profitable for us as business (because we have less client turnover). I'll gladly find you other insurance, at lesser premium (therefore less commission for our agency) so you feel comfortable, and we build trust with your family. Clients love this benefit of our agency and often refer there, friends, family, and neighbors to us for the same service so like any business, good word of mouth is critical. Like a good Financial Advisor, CPA or Attorney, over a period of time recommendations will come up and often change. YOU want to find an agent who operates like this, and has a mindset that you are not just another "number" but wants to cultivate a long term relationship as your trusted insurance advisor.

In fact, I believe that on a daily basis, **our team is one of the most important people you will speak to, from a professional standpoint.** Why do I say this? When your home burns to the ground, whom will you turn to for counsel? If you are seriously hurt in a car accident and unsure what to do, who will be there for you? Should your spouse die unexpectedly, who will help you navigate the waters of filing a life insurance claim? These are all worst-case scenarios, yet real life tells us that these things happen every day, and independent agents all across America are helping their clients with situations just like these; I have personally helped numerous clients through difficult, life-changing situations to make sure their insurance policy was there for them and paid out on the promise.

In fact, our **mission statement at Strategic Insurance is**

"To help families and businesses Prepare, Protect and Recover from life's unexpected events. Move Forward. With Confidence.™"

That is our WHY as a company. That is what drives our leadership team, and it is the commitment we constantly seek to reinforce in our staff. Find a local agent you can truly work with, ask them questions (see Appendix 1), and make sure they are willing to be of service for the long haul. You can find a local independent agent at www.trustedchoice.com. You may think this is "preaching to the choir," in terms of me recommending you find a good insurance agent. The research bears out those clients are often more satisfied have better coverage, with fewer gaps, at an overall lower price than when going online or direct themselves. Insurance is also one of those items that you don't quite know what you are getting, or how your claims service will be **UNTIL something happens.** Insurance agents have a responsibility to be there, and assist in the process (as opposed to going it alone).

Jungle Tip #2- The higher the deductible, the lower the premium. This is true with all insurance. The higher your deductible, the more savings you have on your pricing, as you are taking on some of the risk. The tradeoff can be significant. For example, if you were to raise your home insurance deductible to $2500 from $1000 deductible **you may save on average $400 per year.** The flip side of this is also true, the lower the deductible the higher the premium. While we usually recommend higher deductibles to save clients' money, there are instances and times when clients may want to pay a little more now so as not to have to budget as much out of pocket in the event of a claim. So remember, review and adjust your deductibles, upwards to lower your costs!

1

Brief Overview of Insurance - A Funny Story about Coffee and Boats

DID YOU KNOW that the first insurance contracts go back to the time of the ancient Babylonians in 2nd Century BC? (Neither did I until I started researching this book!). It turns out that early merchants **realized the need to pull together resources and spread the risk, as they travelled treacherous seas.** So instead of one ship with all of the cargo, perhaps three ships would evenly distribute the risk of travelling.

In fact, during this time, merchants often added a surcharge into their cargo to allocate for the chance that their goods would be lost at sea.

Jungle Tip #1- Insurance is the basic idea of spreading the risk. Think about it; how often you have heard "Don't put all your eggs in one basket?" or "There is strength in numbers." This is foundational to insurance. The insurance companies know that if they insure 100 cars for auto insurance or 100 peoples' lives for life insurance, they know pretty confidentially that not ALL 100 cars or people will get into an accident or die that year. By pooling the risk and bringing together all of the premiums, the company can be positive they can pay out for the claims they have in a year and invest the rest to pay for future claims.

Jungle Tip #2- Modern-day insurance goes back to a coffee shop in London in the 17th century.

This leads us to the 17th century and the initiation of Lloyds of London, one of the oldest insurance and financial institutions in the world. If you have never heard of Lloyds of London, they are the granddaddy of insurance. Still in operation today, Lloyds is known as a carrier willing to insure things that no one else will. For example, Lloyds of London insured Lord of the Dance Michael Flattery's legs for a whopping 47 Million dollars at the height of his career! In the 1980s, **Bruce Springsteen insured his voice for 6 million dollars.**[3]

Today, Lloyds of London insures businesses and homes across the world. In fact, in our agency, we have 100s of policies with Lloyds of London insuring everything from vacant homes to businesses.

Back to the 17th-century beginnings, Edward Lloyd in the 1680's opened a coffee house in London on Tower Street. Soon this became a popular spot for ship owners, captains, and sailors who began doing business. So picture over a cup of coffee, not at Starbucks but at Lloyds coffee house, ideas of how to get goods from point A to point B being negotiated. At the same time, the idea of protecting those goods is discussed; hence, maritime insurance was formed much like the ancient Babylonians did in the 2nd Century BC. After Lloyd's death, the Society of Lloyds was formed to continue the underwriting of insurance which blossomed into a global insurance company that is still thriving to this day.[4]

Jungle Tip #3- The impact of a world without insurance-

We take a lot of things for granted today as Americans. I try **to live with an "attitude of gratitude," as Zig Ziglar would say,** but I know I take things for granted. How about you? It's a tough question to ask, especially in a modern-day society, where we get annoyed when our internet doesn't load fast enough on our phone, or we have to wait too

---

3   Odd Things Lloyds of London Insures (http://money.howstuffworks.com/personal-finance/financial-planning/9-odd-things-insured-by-lloyds-of-london.htm#page=8)
4   History of Insurance; Wikipedia (http://en.wikipedia.org/wiki/History_of_insurance)

long in line to fly somewhere, or when the drive through at Chick-Fil-A wraps around the building. (Ok, these are a few of mine, I'll admit!)

Have you ever taken your insurance for granted? I know I have. Take a mental trip with me for a minute. Picture your neighborhood: homes, trees, kids on bikes, basketball hoops in the driveway—you get the picture. Now what if there was a fire so devastating that it destroyed all of the homes in your neighborhood? POOF! One day everything is "apple pie and motherhood" in your favorite area, and then—BAM—13,000 homes burn to the ground. Now let's say that NONE of them were insured. What would the impact be?

Let's travel down that road for a minute. Think about the impact to your family personally. Where would you live? What would you do to replace your belongings? What would you do, both short term and long term? **Would you have the money to self-insure?** Where would you live while your house is being rebuilt? The answer to all of these questions is likely not good. Now what about the ripple effects? Could this affect your job? What about the ability to pay your mortgage? What about the lost opportunity of income for your goods and services to be sold at a local business, e.g., the baker and electronic stores missing out on selling products do to a fire and the impact on the business revenue? It doesn't take long to see the ripple effect that hits the local economy hard.

In fact, this is exactly what happened in the Great Fire of London in 1666. **13,000 homes burned to the ground at great economic loss to a budding city.** At the time, Sir Christopher Wren famously stated that "the development of insurance has gone from a matter of convenience to urgency."[5]

So you may say, "Yea, but that was back when all the buildings were all wood. It's not realistic for MY house or whole neighborhood to burn to the ground." Well, you may be right, but is it possible for a tornado or hurricane to devastate your community? Risks come and

---

5 (Dickson, P. G. M., *The Sun Insurance Office, 1710-1960; The history of two and a half centuries of British insurance,* 1960)

go, but one thing is for sure: there is always the threat of something happening.

Which brings me to the fear factor. I don't like this, and I don't like when people try to scare me into buying something, doing something, or eating (or not eating) something. Do you? Probably not. And insurance, like a lot of industries, can get a bad rap. You likely have a real live person you are talking to that is helping you at some level to make decisions on your insurance plan for your family. Like all industries, there are good and bad insurance advisors, just like there are good and bad dentists, bankers, attorneys, doctors etc.

So I'm not here to be the 'boogie man' and tell you need everything under the sun insured. **In fact, there's some insurance programs and policies I don't like at all (i.e., accident insurance, more about that later).** What the goal of this book will be is to help educate you so you can make informed decisions for your family while getting the best possible price on your family protection plan, and present you the facts of what risks lie out there. **YOU will then be the one to determine what you feel is most appropriate for you and your family.**

Here is a real world, modern-day perspective, on the risks that are insured out there and how the insurance industry has responded. When you look at the 10 Most Catastrophic Events in US history, most of which have occurred in **the last 10 years, you will see that the losses are over 140 Billion dollars, yes, that's Billion- with a B- in terms of the cost of the damage from these events! The impact that insurance provided to help these various communities rebuild and recover has been tremendous.**

THE TEN MOST COSTLY CATASTROPHES, UNITED STATES[6]
($ millions)

Rank	Date	Peril	Estimated insured property losses	
			Dollars when occurred	In 2014 dollars (2)
1	Aug. 2005	Hurricane Katrina	$41,100	$48,383
2	Sep. 2001	Fire, explosion: World Trade Center, Pentagon terrorist attacks	18,779	24,279
3	Aug. 1992	Hurricane Andrew	15,500	23,785
4	Oct. 2012	Hurricane Sandy	18,750	19,307
5	Jan. 1994	Northridge, CA earthquake	12,500	18,345
6	Sep. 2008	Hurricane Ike	12,500	13,639
7	Oct. 2005	Hurricane Wilma	10,300	12,125
8	Aug. 2004	Hurricane Charley	7,475	9,083
9	Sep. 2004	Hurricane Ivan	7,110	8,639
10	Apr. 2011	Flooding, hail and wind including the tornadoes that struck Tuscaloosa and other locations	7,300	7,652

(1) Property losses only. Excludes flood damage covered by the federally administered National Flood Insurance Program.

(2) Adjusted for inflation through 2014 by ISO using the GDP implicit price deflator.

Source: Verisk's Property Claim Services® (PCS®).

Over the last five years, the insurance industry has seen over 850,000 claims—**in lightning claims alone for home insurance in America.**[7] **See chart on next page showing that 100s of millions of dollars paid out for these lightning claims alone!**

---

6   Insurance Info Institute; Top 10 Catastrophic US Claims http://www.iii.org/fact-statistic/catastrophes-us
7   Insurance Information Institute; http://www.iii.org/press-release/number-cost-of-home-owners-insurance-claims-from-lightning-fell-in-2013-dry-conditions-fewer-powerful

HOMEOWNERS INSURANCE CLAIMS AND PAYOUT FOR LIGHTNING LOSSES, 2004-2013

Year	Number of Claims	Value of Claims ($ millions)	Average Cost Per Claim
2004	278,000	$735.5	$2,646
2005	265,700	819.6	3,084
2006	256,000	882.2	3,446
2007	177,100	942.4	5,321
2008	246,200	1,065.5	4,329
2009	185,789	798.1	4,296
2010	213,278	1,033.5	4,846
2011	186,307	952.5	5,112
2012	151,000	969.0	6,400
2013	114,740	673.5	5,869
% change, 2004-2013	-58.7%	-8.4%	121.8%
% change, 2012-2013	-24.0%	-30.5%	-8.3%

Family Protection Points Summary:

- Insurance is expensive and something we don't like to think about. However, the impact on a community, economy and society at large of NOT having insurance can be devastating.
- Remember the "WHY's" in your life as you evaluate your own insurance protection plan.
- Your goal is to protect your family with the best coverage, at the best possible price.

2

Auto Insurance - Price vs. Cost

ZIG ZIGLAR FAMOUSLY said, **"Price is a onetime thing and cost is a lifetime event."** He goes on to share a story about a bike he purchased for his six-year old son. He bought the discount bike for his son instead of spending $30 more for the better Schwinn bike. Well, sure enough it came back to bite him, as the cheaper bike broke down frequently, and he wound up having to spend much more to fix the less expensive option as opposed to spending the additional few dollars up front for the Schwinn bike, which ultimately, would have cost less over the life of the bike.

Jungle Tip #1- Seek value for your auto insurance, NOT just price.

We all have heard the saying, "You get what you pay for." Inherently, we understand this to mean that paying less doesn't often get us the quality we desire as Zig's story above illustrates. And in the light of value, where quality is important, it doesn't make sense to be cheap, especially with your auto insurance.

Why do I start here with this as my first Jungle Tip? Because **you and I are BOMBARDED by advertising for cheap auto insurance thanks to the likes of GEICO, Progressive Direct, and Esurance.** In fact, while typing this chapter and doing research, up popped an ad for Esurance saying, "7 1/2 minutes can save you money on your auto insurance."

First, I'll give you my personal opinion: **I LOVE saving money. I mean, who doesn't, right?** I like getting a deal, and in fact, I often joke that FREE is my favorite four-letter word. But I don't like cheap. Cheap quality—you know, things you spend money on only to realize YOU got the short end of the stick?

Well, this is particularly important with your insurance. Now I'll also tell you, I don't like spending money on my own insurance. **What I do like is the peace of mind and value I get from the protection I have.** I like helping people, and since insurance is so widely held and necessary, it's a way for me to truly assist and serve others. I've always said the value of our agency, and the independent agent at large, is **that we work for YOU, our client and community, not for the insurance company, as we are not tied to any one carrier like a captive company** (e.g., State Farm, Geico, and Progressive Direct).

Now tying this back to auto insurance, statistically speaking, one of your greatest chances of a lawsuit is being at fault in an auto accident. Going back to price vs. cost, do you want the cheapest thing if you are at fault and being sued? Probably not. So here are a few things to look for:

Jungle Tip #2- Minimum 100/300/100 liability limits to protect yourself and your family. Your auto liability is what protects you if you are at fault in an accident and hurt the people in the other car. It also includes damage for the other car itself and any other property you damaged.

The **100 stands for $100,000 worth of liability protection if there is one person in the other car who is hurt.** Now if there are multiple people in the car or multiple cars involved, you would have a maximum of $300,000 (which is what the 300 stands for). The last 100 stands for $100,000 in any damage you did to another person's property or vehicle.

Why 100/300/100? This limit is regarded by most financial and insurance experts as good coverage for the average family. In fact depending on your assets you likely should have higher than 100/300 and an umbrella. More on that later in the book.

Financial experts often recommend that the normal limits of 10/20 or even 25/50 are simply not enough. In fact financial advisor, Ray Martin, penned an article for CBS MoneyWatch in 2013 stating "why you need higher liability limits." [8]

Depending on the state you live in, there are statutory limits that are required for your auto insurance. In my state of Florida, the scary thing is **that the state doesn't require you to have liability insurance at all!** They just want a minimum of 10k for property damage, and the minimum coverage for liability insurance is 10k.

So going back to price vs. cost, and truly understanding the value, I can tell you as an agent firsthand that I see a **lot of clients that have 10/20/10 liability insurance.** While they think they are getting a good deal in saving money by having lower limits (than say 100/300) what happens if they get into an accident and seriously hurt someone?

Most of them have good income and enough assets to need much higher protection than 10k liability protection. Think about this; how far does 10k go these days for medical bills? Not to minimize 10k—it's still a lot of money, but **if you hurt someone while driving a two-ton Ford Explorer SUV, how far is 10k going to go for their medical bills?**

We all know that healthcare costs are high and only getting higher. I hear they charge $300 for some band aids in hospitals! Ok that is a joke, but not that far off. **The point to consider is the VALUE of protecting your families ASSETS and 100/300/100 is a good place to start.** If you have assets to protect and you go through 10k of liability coverage, you will then be forced to pay out of pocket for your damages to the other person.

I want to take a minute to layout all of the liability options that you usually see an auto insurance company offer.

Remember the first number is for liability damage that you caused if there is one person in the car. The middle number provides liability protection if there are multiple people in the car or more than one car

---

8 CBS MoneyWatch; Why you Need More Liability Insurance http://www.cbsnews.com/news/why-you-need-more-liability-insurance/

involved with injuries, and the last number represents any damage you did to the other car or other property:

Standard Limits of liability:

$10,000/$20,000/$10,000 $100,000/$300,000/$100,000

$25,000/$50,000/$25,000 $250,000/$500,000/$100,000

$50,000/$100,000/$50,000 $500,000/$500,000/$100,000

While we recommend 100/300/100 it's important to note that **IF you simply cannot afford that high of liability you are still better off with 50/100/50 or 25/50/25** than settling for 10/20 as the lowest limits. Often times the price difference between 10/20 and 100/300 is a few hundred dollars every 6 months (assuming a good driving history). Also be aware that one of the rating factors that insurance companies use is your prior limit history. This means that insurance companies look more favorably at higher limits than lower limits as they have research to show that people with higher limits of liability are less likely to cause accidents, and be more cautious on the roads. Therefore you actually get a pricing tier credit for having a higher limit. The reverse of this is true as well in that having low limits of liability (i.e. 10/20/10) over a long period of time puts you at a higher rated tier.

By the way, this is not to say that 100/300/100 with Geico or Esurance is bad coverage (if you have those companies). The concern is often that you have no one to advise you with true professional experience and knowledge (most direct carriers operate in a large call center environment trying to make a sale at all cost on the first call), whereas a local independent agent is often looking to get to know you and your family and build a long-term relationship with you to be a trusted advisor. That's what we strive for at Strategic Insurance (my agency), to be our clients' trusted advisor and tell them not just what they want to hear but what they need to hear.

The higher liability coverage is often not that much more expensive than the barebones coverage. In general you want to be mindful of your assets and income, and as your income and assets increase, so should your liability protection. Often times we recommend when doing an umbrella liability **policy to protect your net worth**. Again, more on that to come.

Real life impact story: I got into the insurance industry right out of college in 2002. In late 2004, we had a truly a tragic scenario regarding auto liability coverage for a client at the first agency I worked for. We had a business owner client of ours who killed a man on a motorcycle not more than two blocks from my old office—tragic. One Sunday morning, she got up like any other day and not thinking something tragic would happen. By definition, a claim is sudden and accidental. The ripple effects were felt throughout our community, as the man was a soccer coach at a local university. Although we had recommended multiple times for her to have higher limits and a liability umbrella, she did not. The carrier paid policy limits that week, and the client was then faced with not only the emotional tragedy of killing someone, but the financial loss of having to defend and pay out of pocket for what was likely to be a substantial lawsuit. The takeaway is be wise and adequately protect yourself. If you don't know how much coverage you should have, do a review of your assets and liabilities as well as seek counsel from your insurance agent, financial advisor, or attorney.

Jungle Tip #3- Check for all the discounts you are eligible for as well as driving-based discounts. Now how to save money on the auto insurance. Some of the most common discounts now are EFT (i.e., monthly auto draft of your bank account), paperless discount (i.e., everything gets sent to you electronically), paid in full discount, multi-car discount, homeowner discount, low mileage discount, and good-student discount for your kids' good grades (usually 3.0 or B average and higher). Additionally, carriers will usually give discounts for car alarms and anti-lock brakes, so make sure to check those on your policies. Some companies like Progressive Insurance. In full disclosure we represent Progressive as they also have an independent insurance agent distribution model in addition to direct to consumer. You can see many of the companies we represent at our website, www.GetStrategicIns.com.

Many companies offer sizable discounts for paid in full premiums. It's **not unusual to see a 10% discount for a policy paid in full.** I recommend if you can afford to do this option, or even put it on a credit card (assuming low or no interest rates) and pay that off each month you will be saving yourself money in the long run.

Lately, within the last two years, one of the hot **new discounts available is a driver-based ratings discount.** Progressive Insurance was the first to pioneer this technology. The Snapshot Discount by Progressive leverages technology to see your driving patterns and behavior.[9] It monitors the time of day you drive, the average speed you drive, and the amount of hard brakes you do. Think about it. If you drive really fast late at night, do you think you are going to have more risk of an accident? Very likely so! But if I don't drive as late, or as fast, or as much, would my chances of having an accident be less? Again, very likely so!

Thanks to the increases in technology, we can now determine and gather this data. Remember, insurance companies are all about matching premium to risk (i.e., how much you pay to how risky you or what is being insured is). On average, the **clients in our agency have seen approximately a 17% reduction in their premium after doing the Snapshot check. Some have seen up to 30%.** Many carriers are now offering something similar, so for all those people who say, "I'm a good driver; I should get a better rate," now is your chance to prove it.

Understanding the rest of your auto policy:

Uninsured motorist coverage. Ok, so we talked about protecting your assets in the event of an accident when you're at fault with your auto liability insurance and how to check for all of your discounts. Now what about the other guy when they are at fault and hurt YOU? Well, that's what uninsured motorist coverage does; it protects you

---

9   Progressive Snapshot Discount; http://www.progressive.com/snapshot

in an accident when the other person is at fault and does not have enough coverage to take care of your medical bills and other damages. Think about this: in my home state of Florida, in the Tampa Bay area where we live, **almost 30% of all drivers have no coverage or are underinsured (meaning the other driver doesn't have enough coverage for your damages).** Yikes! So if one of these drivers hurts you, your uninsured motorist would kick in to take care of your medical bills and potential lost wages. We recommend 100/300 liability, giving you $100,000 if you are in the car yourself or $300,000 if multiple people are in your car.

We often get asked, "Why do I need uninsured motorist coverage if I have health insurance?" Good question. The simple answer is **uninsured motorist covers MORE than just medical bills.** One of the biggest sections of uninsured motorist damage includes pain and suffering or better known as punitive damages. So if you got hurt in an accident and had permanent injuries or injuries that changed your lifestyle, **you could certainly make a case for punitive damages to be paid out through uninsured motorist coverage.** I know of a person who was rear ended and has permanent tingling in his hands; picture those uncomfortable "pins and needle" sensation you get when a body part falls asleep. Yea that's annoying and painful. Well that is a classic case where uninsured motorist coverage would come in to play as the person who rear ended this individual had no liability coverage. The other question we get asked a lot is, "So you are telling me that I have to pay for MORE insurance because most people are UNDER insured, or worse have no insurance? That's not fair." I agree, but we all know life isn't fair. **The reality is uninsured motorist coverage is the best way to protect yourself against the majority of motorists on the road who have low limits of liability coverage or NO insurance at all.**

Now a lot of people will call our agency, and when asked, "What kind of coverage do they currently have?" often they respond, "Full coverage." Ever heard someone say that before or refer to your coverage like that yourself? Well, what they mean is coverage for the vehicle (i.e., comprehensive and collision coverage), that's typically what they are referring to as "full coverage." **Comprehensive coverage is**

13

basically anything other than an accident: things like theft, fire, or flooding. Collision is your car being hit (or hitting someone) in an accident, defined as an accident or upset to the vehicle typically.

The takeaway here is to make SURE you know what your deductibles are and verify whether you have the coverage you want or need for your vehicle. Often times, I've met with clients who were referred to me, and when I review their current coverage, they are shocked to learn that they did not have either collision or comprehensive coverage. In addition to knowing what your deductibles are, **look at increasing your deductibles not only to save money but to prevent future rate increases from filing small claims.** I still see some clients with a $100 to $250 deductible for their comprehensive or collision, which is the amount of out of pocket they are responsible for in a claim. I would **look at least at $500 or $1000 deductible for your comprehensive and collision coverage.**

Personal Injury Protection:

Depending the state you live in you may be governed by personal injury protection (or PIP) for short. You will also here this referred to as "no fault" insurance coverage. Currently 12 states in the US have the personal injury protection requirement including states like Florida, Michigan, New York and Michigan. **PIP coverage ensures that regardless of who is at fault in an accident the insurance policy should provide for medical bills up to $10,000 for an injured party.** The idea behind this is a way of cutting down on frivolous lawsuits. In other states you have tort liability the at-fault party is responsible for paying for all damages.[10]

So if you are in a state like Florida, bottom line you have to have PIP. The big takeaway here is to **watch out for deductibles on your PIP.** Often times I see clients who come to me with a prior insurance company (often a direct company) with a $1000 PIP deductible.

---

10 Auto Owners Insurance; No fault vs. Tort Liability http://www.auto-owners.com/our-products/car-insurance/resource-center/insurance/no-fault-car-insurance

That deductible on your PIP saves VERY little on your premium. We are talking a few dollars (not hundreds of dollars). To me it's not worth it to have to pay dollar one in an accident for your OWN medical bills, so the minimal savings do not justify the increased risk out of pocket that YOU face. **IF you have a deductible on your PIP, remove it!** Personal injury protection can also cover items such as lost wages, and death in an accident. The benefit usually maxes out at $10,000 for all benefits that would be included, so check your policy for complete details.

Rental Car Coverage and Towing

Lastly, I **recommend rental car coverage and towing coverage.** I see this coverage missed a lot. People think at times that because they have a new car and the dealer provides them with a car when their car is in the shop, that they don't need rental car coverage. **That is incorrect, as the dealer is only covering the car in the event of mechanical breakdown or routine maintenance.** If your car is in an accident or stolen, they don't provide rental coverage. Going to rent a car for 2 to 3 weeks can get very expensive very fast, often with bills well over $1000. Rental car coverage provides you with a reimbursement per day for a rental car. I recommend $40 per day up to $1200; you can certainly do more based on the type of vehicle and rates you would expect to pay for a rental car in your area. This is a great value add and often costs less than $10 per 6 months for the coverage. Towing coverage is usually less than $5 every 6 months and covers things like a flat tire, breakdown of any kind needing a tow or locking your keys in your car. Depending on the company some of them have a service like AAA where you can call them directly for them to come out, otherwise keep your receipt and the company will reimburse you. I know many people, like and use AAA for this. Depending on **your AAA membership you are usually only covered for 2 incidents per year with a limited mileage amount on the tow, so I believe this is a great coverage for a small price tag that you should consider towing coverage.** It often gets missed.

Family Protection Point Summary:

Go get your auto insurance declaration page right now. Go ahead, I'll wait :-). Seriously, go get it and review it. Most people get it in the mail and throw it in a file. Or they get it via email, scan for their ID cards, and delete it. Now go review your coverage.

- How **much liability and uninsured motorist coverage do you have?**
- Have you made sure you have all the discounts discussed earlier?
- What are your comp and collision deductibles? And **do you have rental car coverage?**

To get more info on this subject and a comprehensive review of your auto insurance, email me at Doug@GetStrategicIns.com.

3

Home Sweet Home - Protecting your house

FOR MOST AMERICANS, your home is your biggest asset. While home ownership is down, **approximately 2/3 of all American's own their home.**[11]

Now I want you to picture your first home buying experience. For some, it was likely a time of excitement, anticipation, and stress. Buying a home has a lot of moving parts; you're thinking about packing, moving, new lawn or pool service, changing your mailing address, arranging financing, doing inspections etc.

Often, your homeowner's insurance is an afterthought. Perhaps your realtor or mortgage person gave you a few names of insurance agents telling you to get insurance for closing or maybe they provided you quotes from their referral partners directly. **I realize insurance by its very nature is not sexy, fun, or exciting.** But it is so important (as we discussed previously the economic impact of insurance) and here will look at 3 Jungle Tips to understand when looking for home insurance, whether for your first home buying experience, or reviewing your current coverage.

---

11   Bloomberg Homeownership; (http://www.bloomberg.com/news/2014-04-29/u-s-homeownership-rate-falls-to-the-lowest-since-1995.html).

Jungle Tip #1- Understanding your property and replacement cost coverage

There a many parts to your home insurance coverage that we will cover later in the chapter, but if your home is your biggest asset, then the dwelling or building coverage is the most important part of your home insurance plan.

Your **building coverage is the maximum amount of coverage that the insurance company will give you to rebuild your home in the event of a total loss.** This coverage is usually referred to on an insurance declarations page as "Dwelling Coverage A." For example, if you have a home insurance policy with building coverage of $250,000 that represents the most the insurance company will pay to rebuild.

Here are important points on that building coverage to correct myths out there that we hear all the time:

Myth #1- "I only owe $150,000 on the house or my house is only worth $200,000 so I should only need that much coverage? Just enough to cover my loan, or what my house would sell for, right?"

Answer: You need (and want) **coverage to REBUILD your home**. So let's run through the scenario with some numbers—sound like fun? Ok, so let's say you buy a house for $300,000 but put $200,000 down and only owe $100,000 on it. Now let's say you've got 2200 heated sq. feet, 3 beds, 2 bathrooms, with a 2 car garage, and to REBUILD the house in current dollars without depreciation (more on this in a minute), a total of $275,000 is needed to rebuild the same 2200 sq. foot house with like, kind and quality materials.

Now, if you only take out $100,000 insurance coverage, thinking, "Well, that's all I need for the mortgage," **you would be sorely mistaken.** And if your house were destroyed, you would also be out $175,000 in rebuild costs! Fortunately, most insurance policies will not allow you to underinsure. By definition, they will want you to have "replacement cost."

So what is **replacement cost? Replacement cost is the amount you need to rebuild your house in today's dollars with the same like, kind and quality of construction materials as you currently have in your**

home before the claim occurred. So hardwood floors are replaced with hardwood, siding with siding, bricks with bricks, granite counter tops with granite counter tops. The big thing here is that no depreciation is factored in. This is especially important on older homes. As homes age, the MATERIALS depreciate so this is especially crucial.

Make sure your house is properly insured at the replacement cost. If you are underinsured, you can face penalties in the event of a claim. I'll spare you the long boring math (for those of you long boring math types, email me at Doug@GetStrategicIns.com and I will email you an example of a co-insurance penalty), but basically, since you are underinsured and have a claim, you are penalized. Big time.

Again, with our quick example from above, let's say you only had $100,000 in coverage and had a $50,000 claim due to a fire. Since you were underinsured, you may only get paid $25,000. Not good.

Ask your agent to do an updated replacement cost estimate. As agents, we have specialized software that is designed by engineers and updated quarterly to assess how much coverage you need on your house based on all of the features such as year built, sq. footage, number of beds and bathrooms, quality of construction, and special features such as pool, screen enclosure, and fireplace. Based on these assessments, you would have a good idea of how much it will cost to rebuild. Note you as the client always have the final say as it is YOUR insurance and your dollars being spent. It can also be a good idea to review the replacement cost estimate provided by a certified appraiser or get the advice of a local builder in your area to see what a reasonable price per square foot for rebuild is of your style home.

Real life story: We are currently working with a client who has his home insurance who had $550,000 of coverage on his house. He bought an older home in a nice area of Tampa and completely remodeled it. He put $250,000 into the house to remodel it. When we did our most recent protection review with our client, we uncovered this and immediately updated so he was adequately insured. What if this didn't happen and the client had a total loss? I can tell you—they would not be happy. **Let your agent or insurance company know if**

you have updated your house and done remodeling so that your insurance can be accurate.

Jungle Tip #2- Higher deductibles, wind mitigation credits, and monitored alarm are the biggest keys to saving money on your home insurance.

In my home state of Florida, home insurance is among the most expensive in the country, with average premiums hovering around $2,000/year.[12] Not surprisingly, most of the Gulf Coast states that face the risk of hurricanes have the highest insurance premiums.

It is staggering when you consider that the top 10 most devastating hurricanes of all time have cost the insurance industry **over 120 BILLION in paid claims! And seven of them have directly affected Florida within the last 15 years.**

See the chart below from the Insurance Information Institute[13]

THE TEN MOST COSTLY HURRICANES IN THE UNITED STATES ($ millions)

Rank	Date	Location	Hurricane	Estimated insured loss (2)	
				Dollars when occurred	In 2014 dollars (3)
1	Aug. 25-30, 2005	AL, FL, GA, LA, MS, TN	Hurricane Katrina	$41,100	$48,383
2	Aug. 24-26, 1992	FL, LA	Hurricane Andrew	15,500	23,785
3	Oct. 28-31, 2012	CT, DC, DE, MA, MD, ME, NC, NH, NJ, NY, OH, PA, RI, VA, VT, WV	Hurricane Sandy	18,750	19,307
4	Sep. 12-14, 2008	AR, IL, IN, KY, LA, MO, OH, PA, TX	Hurricane Ike	12,500	13,639
5	Oct. 24, 2005	FL	Hurricane Wilma	10,300	12,125

12   Average cost of Home insurance; (http://www.valuepenguin.com/average-cost-of-home-owners-insurance#least).
13   10 Most Costly US Hurricanes- http://www.iii.org/fact-statistic/hurricanes

Rank	Date	Location	Hurricane	Estimated insured loss (2)	
				Dollars when occurred	**In 2014 dollars (3)**
6	Aug. 13-14, 2004	FL, NC, SC	Hurricane Charley	7,475	9,083
7	Sep. 15-21, 2004	AL, DE, FL, GA, LA, MD, MS, NC, NJ, NY, OH, PA, TN, VA, WV	Hurricane Ivan	7,110	8,639
8	Sep. 17-22, 1989	GA, NC, PR, SC, UV, VA	Hurricane Hugo	4,195	7,055
9	Sep. 20-26, 2005	AL, AR, FL, LA, MS, TN, TX	Hurricane Rita	5,627	6,624
10	Sep. 3-9, 2004	FL, GA, NC, NY, SC	Hurricane Frances	4,595	5,583

(1) Includes hurricanes occurring through 2014.

(2) Property coverage only. Excludes flood damage covered by the federally administered National Flood Insurance Program.

(3) Adjusted for inflation through 2014 by ISO using the GDP implicit price deflator.

Source: Verisk's Property Claim Services® (PCS®).

So we all know home insurance is expensive, especially in the Southeast United States. The question is, "What do we do about it to get good coverage at reasonable rates?"

Here are 3 specific things you can do to help find the best rate. Number one, get a wind mitigation inspection. I repeat: **GET A WIND MITIGATION INSPECTION. It's that important—period.** If you do nothing else other than get a wind mitigation inspection you will be very happy you read this book. After being in the insurance business for over 10 years, I can tell you without a doubt that wind mitigation discounts are the biggest tool to save money on your home insurance. And I'm talking some serious money. First, what is it? A wind mitigation inspection is a specific inspection done on the roof of your home to assess its overall strength and likelihood of holding up well in the event of strong wind. It looks at how the roof is attached to the truss, how many nails are used in attaching the roof, the shape of the roof, and several other factors. Why does this help save you money you ask? **The wind mitigation report is proof to the insurance company about the strength and durability of your roof.** Knowing that a stronger roof will likely have less damage in the event of high wind, the companies can justify a discount and in fact want to insure homes with excellent roofs as they realize they will likely pay out less in claims in the event of high wind. How much of a discount you say? **The discount for a newer roof with several features that are applicable to the wind mitigation inspection form can result in anywhere from a 10% to 40% discount. It's huge.**

On my own house, my wind mitigation saves me almost $1,900/year. Yes, almost $1900/year. This inspection, by the way, usually costs less than $100 to do by a licensed home inspector. I've literally seen a wind mitigation discount cut a premium in half, from $4,000 to $2,000. We recommend this to ALL of our clients and future clients because of the impact. Note that the inspection does not impact your eligibility; it is only for rating purposes. Go get one if you don't have one already.

The second specific thing you can do to save money on your homeowners insurance is increase your deductible, which I mentioned previously is a key to lowering any insurance premium. It's important to know that most home insurance policies today have two deductibles. One is an "all other peril" deductible, and the other is usually a hurricane deductible. The **all other peril deductible is truly for ANYTHING other than hurricanes.** This can be fire, theft, lightning strike, or water leakage. The most common deductibles are $500, $1000, and $2500. So by going from, say, a $1000 deductible to a $2500 deductible, you may save $200 to $400 per year. This is a significant savings on most policies. Note that you can also increase your hurricane deductible, which is usually a percentage deductible of your homes building coverage (which appears on your declarations page under, Coverage A), at either 2% or 5% of the building amount. Inherently because damage from hurricanes is usually your biggest risk, I'm always cautious when talking with a client who may want a 5% deductible over a 2% deductible. There is some savings, but it is usually not as much as increasing the all other peril deductible. This is certainly an option for some people who are comfortable with a higher out of pocket cost for hurricane damage and again could save anywhere from $100 to $200/year.

Lastly, if you have a central station monitored alarm, make SURE you see the discount on your home insurance declarations page and verify with your agent or insurance company that you are getting a discount if you have an alarm. Note the alarm has to be CENTRAL station monitored (i.e., Brinks, ADT, etc.), where you pay for a service that reports to either the police or fire department in the event of an emergency. Lots of people have monitored alarms and don't always think to notify their agent or the insurance company. This discount can save you anywhere from $150 to $400/year depending on the carrier. I have one last note on the alarm: **make sure that if it is monitored for fire as well as burglary that you notify your agent.** You will need to substantiate the alarm monitoring with a certificate that you can request from your alarm company to get the discount.

Other discounts to review are a **home/flood insurance discount.** While fewer and fewer companies are doing home/auto discounts (especially in the Southeast), several companies are now writing flood insurance in addition to home insurance and are willing to give you a discount on the home insurance to incentivize you to do the flood insurance. You may also see some companies offer a managed services claims discount. **Both of these discounts can be anywhere from 3 to 10% depending on the company.** One note on the managed services claims discount is that the program is where the home insurance company has pre-determined contractors who they work with for their claims handling. The goal of this is to expedite claims for clients, and keep costs low. While this sounds great, you are giving up control of picking WHO will be the one to repair your home so make sure to do further research and that you are comfortable with contractors for this discount. Lastly, some companies will give small discounts for 55 and older, as well as gated community discounts.

By doing these items listed above and reviewing you are getting all of your discounts, you can usually save significantly on your home insurance without cutting into any major coverage, thus obtaining a good value for the price.

Jungle Tip #3- Shop around. Smokey Robinson said it best: "My momma told me you better shop around." This goes back to our Preface: one of the biggest takeaways from surviving the insurance jungle is to **find a good independent agent who can review the marketplace for you**, especially on your homeowner's insurance, where the endorsements and options can be complex. Part of the value independent agents bring to the table is the strength they have in representing multiple companies. At Strategic Insurance Services we have 17 home insurance companies to choose from. Should you be in an area of the country where Nationwide Insurance or All State issue home insurance, all they can typically offer is coverage from their own corporate company. They are excellent companies—don't get me wrong—and should you currently be insured with a large carrier like an Allstate, USAA, or State Farm, I'm not telling you to run out and switch. What I am telling **you is to be realistic in knowing that all they offer is one company, and with the dynamics of the property market, it's likely that over a period of time, they will not be the most competitive** from either a coverage or pricing standpoint. So find an agent who represents multiple companies and ask them how many companies they have, who they recommend, and why.

The goal would be to align yourself with an agent who will do this for you year after year. At our agency, we do Annual Protection Reviews by contacting our clients 60 days before their insurance renews to do a review of their coverage and company comparison of other options. It is always a great feeling to go to a client with a recommendation that adds value and protection to them while saving them money and for our clients to know we are truly looking out for their best interest. If you are interested in a review of your own policies and would like a market comparison of the other insurance company options, email me at Info@GetStrategicIns.com and put "Jungle Insurance Review" in the subject line.

4

Health Insurance - How ACA has changed the landscape forever

Wherever you stand from a political point of view, there is **no doubt that the Affordable Care Act, aka "Obamacare," has changed the landscape for health insurance in America forever.** The changes are dramatic, can be complicated, and come with a host of long-term unknowns.

One of the challenges of writing a book like this, a guide for insurance for the consumer, is that this is a snapshot in time. As the law evolves, new challenges arise so the goal of this chapter will be "view from 30,000 feet." The health insurance industry is going through a period of uncertainty, and shake up that has not been seen in over 50 years as a result of ACA.

The goal of this chapter is not to speculate or pontificate about what the long-term impact will be of the ACA law. At the time, we are headed into open enrollment for only the 2nd year as we turn the corner to 2016. The goal for this chapter, really as all of the chapters, is to provide real-world, practical information you and your family can use, focusing on how to maximize your benefits.

Jungle Tip #1- Pre Existing conditions have been eliminated. Previously, when clients would call me looking for health insurance, one of the biggest hurdles was a client who had a pre-existing health condition. Health insurance was based primarily on what was in your medical records, and depending on your condition, the company could either exclude a condition (e.g., a back injury that would be excluded on your policy), charge more premium for a condition (e.g., increased cost due to prescriptions), or decline you altogether (e.g., diabetes would make you ineligible).

In the new **ACA laws, there is NO medical underwriting.** That's right—NO questions about your health. **This is a good thing in my opinion.** There is nothing worse than being sick and not being able to get coverage, and nothing that was more challenging as an agent wanting to help an individual or family who needed the insurance and was willing to pay for it, but couldn't get the coverage due to their health conditions.

It still surprises people who are unaware that the new health insurance laws do not ask health questions and that you cannot be excluded from coverage due to your health (or lack of). So go ahead and apply without fear.

The rating factors that do go into the health insurance premiums have changed as well. Under the new ACA laws the only rating factors insurance companies can use are:

1. **Your age-** We all know that the older you are, the more likely you are to have health issues, and therefore higher medical care costs. As a result, it makes sense that the older you are the more expensive your premium. With the changes to the laws, they have set **that the oldest rate charges for premium can be no more than three times higher than the youngest rates**. That means several ages are squeezed into 3 age bands, whether you are 18 or 64. Over time could be problematic as it will not reflect as accurate of rates which could lump you in

a higher banded rate than need be, but for now this is how the government is regulating the rates.
2. **Zip code-** Where you live affects your rates due to competition, local regulation, and the networks that the insurance companies have established with hospitals and doctors. For example, a rural area may see fewer hospitals and doctors choices due to its location which could impact the options for insurance that people in that area would have as well as the price the insurance company charges for the insurance.
3. **Tobacco-** Insurance companies can charge up to 50% more for people who use tobacco. **This is yet one more reason to quit smoking!**[14]

Jungle Tip #2- Plans are now established based on a metallic scale from Bronze to Platinum. Part of the goal of health care reform was to make health insurance simpler. Whether that has happened or not is a matter of opinion by the American consumer. Given the amount of notices, ongoing changes and historic level of government involvement clearly certain aspects of the new health insurance is far from simple. However, I will say as a seasoned agent, that the streamlining of plans based a metallic code (similar to medals in the Olympics) **does make coverage comparisons easier.**

For example, Bronze plans will have lower premiums with higher out of pocket costs, while Platinum plans will have lower out of pocket costs but higher premiums. In general, Silver plans will be somewhere between the middle of the pack in terms of balancing premium per month and the out of pocket costs.

"Plans in the Marketplace are primarily separated into 4 health plan categories — Bronze, Silver, Gold, or Platinum — based on the percentage the plan pays of the average overall cost of providing essential health benefits to members. The plan category you choose affects the total amount you'll likely spend for essential health benefits during the year. The percentages the plans will spend, on average, are 60% (Bronze), 70% (Silver), 80% (Gold), and 90% (Platinum). This isn't the same as

---

14 How health insurers can set their pricing; https://www.healthcare.gov/lower-costs/how-plans-set-your-premiums/

coinsurance, in which you pay a specific percentage of the cost of a specific service." [15]

Jungle Tip #3- Check if you are eligible for a subsidy. The government is also willing to put money towards the cost of health insurance for individuals and families depending on household income and the number of dependents in the household.

As of the 2016 enrollment period, you would general qualify for a subsidy if:

- You are single and yearly income is less than $47,000 per year
- There are two people in the household and yearly income is less than $63,000 per year
- There are three people in the household and yearly income is less than $79,000 per year
- There are four people in the household and yearly income is less than $95,400 per year[16]

I cannot stress enough **how important it is to actually apply on www.healthcare.gov to determine your subsidy.** While there are several subsidy calculators out there, including one from the Kaiser Family (*http://kff.org/interactive/subsidy-calculator/*). It's important to understand that this is JUST an estimate. I can say from real-world experience working with lots of clients that sometimes the subsidy estimate was higher and sometime it was lower. Until you go through the application on www.healthcare.gov and the government pulls info from the IRS database, you cannot be assured of a subsidy.

Health insurance is one of the most necessary and important protections you and your family can have against a catastrophic financial loss due to poor health. So many people have gone bankrupt or have had to go into foreclosure on their home due to unforeseen health expenditures while having no health insurance.
We have all seen reports and heard stories of incredibly high medical bills, figures that we can't even fathom. According to an article from the National Business Group on Health Report:

---

15 Health Plan Category Listings; https://www.healthcare.gov/glossary/health-plan-categories/
16 Subsidy info for health plans; https://www.healthcare.gov/lower-costs/qualifying-for-lower-costs/

"**The average total cost of a severe heart attack—including direct and indirect costs—is about $1 million**. Direct costs include charges for hospitals, doctors, and prescription drugs, while the indirect costs include lost productivity and time away from work. The average cost of a less severe heart attack is about $760,000. Amortized over 20 years, that's $50,000 per year for a severe heart attack and $38,000 per year for a less severe heart attack."[17]

However you look at it, the numbers can certainly be daunting. Therefore, it's important that you **know what your deductible and co-insurance are for your health plan**. Your deductible is the amount you are responsible for before the insurance begins to pay. The co-insurance is the percentage that the insurance company splits costs of your medical bills with you AFTER the deductible is met. The most common co-insurance you will see is 80/20 co-insurance, meaning after the deductible is met, the insurance company will pick up 80% of the bill and you will pay 20% of the bill, until you have met your out of pocket maximum. The **deductible plus your co-insurance totals your max out of pocket costs** and these are capped by **ACA at approximately $6350 for an individual and $12,600 for a family.** Your maximum out of pocket is the worst case financial burden in a calendar year that you would incur. The key word in that sentence is "calendar" year. This means if you have a serious health issue in November and blow thru your deductible and co-insurance you will start scratch at the beginning of January as that is a new calendar year and you would be subject to new deductibles and co-insurance. Here's a quick example: Let's say you have your appendix removed and the bill is $15,000 total. Assume you have a $4000 deductible you will pay the first $4000 of bills to the party who is billing you whether it be the hospital, doctor, or some other party. NOW once you have paid your 4k, another bill comes in at $1000 from the surgeon. Your insurance company should pay $800 (or 80%) and you would pay $200 (or 20%). Once you hit $6350 total payments out of pocket your medical bills should be covered at 100% for the rest

---

17 How much would a heart attack cost you; http://www.cbsnews.com/news/how-much-would-a-heart-attack-cost-you/

of the calendar year, with the exception of co-payments for doctor's office visits and prescription coverage. Of course this is just an example so please check your plan for full details as various plans may differ.

Your **max out of pocket is one of the most important parts to your health insurance and one that most people do not pay attention to until it's too late**. When people call me asking for health insurance, most times they want to know about their costs for prescriptions and doctor's office visits.

While this is important, it's not nearly as important as how the plan works with regards to major claims.

It's important to note that while there is increasing flexibility for the underwriting of health insurance with no medical underwriting and opportunities for government subsidies to help with payments, there is a drawback under the new healthcare laws.

Family Protection Point: YOU CAN ONLY ENROLL for health insurance during open enrollment. Under the ACA laws, now you can ONLY enroll during open enrollment, which was from November 15th 2014 to February 15th 2015 this past year. This is the time of year when you can apply without any life-qualifying event to secure coverage. What's a life-qualifying event you ask? Well that is the only other way you can apply for health insurance.

Examples of qualifying life events include:

- Marriage or divorce
- Having a baby, adopting a child, or placing a child for adoption or foster care
- Moving your residence, gaining citizenship, leaving incarceration
- Losing other health coverage due to losing job-based coverage, the end of an individual policy plan year in 2014, COBRA expiration, aging off a parent's plan, losing eligibility for Medicaid or CHIP, and similar circumstances.
- **Important:** Voluntarily ending coverage doesn't qualify you for a special enrollment period. Neither does losing coverage that doesn't qualify as minimum essential coverage.

- For people already enrolled in Marketplace coverage: Having a change in income or household status that affects eligibility for premium tax credits or cost-sharing reductions[18]

Before the ACA laws, clients could call me at ANY time during the year and apply for coverage. The challenges then were any current health conditions that would prevent you from being able to get coverage and also cost. Now **the primary challenge is really procrastination.** While cost is always an issue, for certain income levels, there is the opportunity for subsidies. People need to understand that they have a limited time to apply, outside of some unique life qualifying events.

Plans are dynamic and changing from year to year as the industry is getting used to the new normal of ACA. The biggest challenge the healthcare law will face, according to most economic and financial experts who have examined the law and are projecting the implications of the law now and into the future, **will be the ability to get young people to sign up for health insurance.** We know that the government for the first time ever has the authority to tax people for NOT complying with the ACA law. You may ask, "How would one violate this law?" Well **it's as simple as someone not purchasing health insurance**. This is known as the individual mandate and can be as. The maximum penalty is the national average cost of a Bronze plan.[19] The goal is to get **high as 2% of your adjusted gross earnings, or $325 whichever is higher** younger people age 35 and younger who have never had insurance before to sign up for plans. In the word picture of the "carrot and the stick" to motivate people, the government is using the "stick" here to impact the behavior of younger people who traditionally have not carried coverage under the idea that they are healthy. Since the new ACA laws passed, with no medical underwriting, the healthcare system is America is **being stretched to the breaking point as many older, sick American's are signing up.** To offset the costs of the claims

---

18 Life qualifying events for special enrollment periods; https://www.healthcare.gov/coverage-outside-open-enrollment/special-enrollment-period/

19 Tax penalty for not having health insurance; https://www.healthcare.gov/fees-exemptions/fee-for-not-being-covered/

of these citizens the insurance companies need younger clients who are paying regularly but not filing much in the way of claims; it is the classic balancing act.

In terms of shopping, all of the major companies are good to look at including United Healthcare Insurance, Humana, Cigna, Aetna, Coventry and Blue Cross Blue Shield. Of course your local independent agent who does health insurance can be a resource to you as well.

In summary, health insurance is in a state of great change but also great opportunity for Americans who may not have had coverage before. Make sure you check updates on www.healthcare.gov for open enrollment dates and guidelines surrounding options to enroll outside of open enrollment.

5

Disability Insurance - More than just a "Quack Quack"

IF YOU CAN'T already tell by the 5th-chapter title, I'm trying to have a little fun and breathe some life into the insurance business; well, here's my last and best chance.

Quick—think "Quack Quack Quack." What insurance company commercial comes to mind? AFLAC! Can you hear the famed AFLAC mascot quacking and then saying, "AFLAC." Well the pitch men that the American Family Life and Assurance Company (AFLAC, sounds much better doesn't it) sure hit a homerun with the most famous duck since Donald and Daffy.

So why am I beginning this chapter with AFLAC? Well, this is the chapter where we are going to **talk about protecting your biggest asset.** Now picture your biggest asset. Your home? Your savings and investments? Both are good answers—but wrong. Really, when you break it down, your largest asset is **YOUR ABILITY TO EARN money both now AND in the future.** So the AFLAC duck is talking about protecting your income.

Ok, so I know what you are thinking right now. "Yeah yeah, that's great, but I'm healthy as a horse. I eat well and exercise. Nothing is going to happen to me." Well, God willing, I hope nothing serious happens to you. At its most basic form, insurance is managing risk and helping people recover from unexpected life events (hence where our SIS mission comes into play). It's also a lot about "fact and not feeling." The insurance industry spends an exorbitant amount of money to chronicle and research almost every part of life to develop statistical trends with which they can make assessments of the risk they are insuring. You may have heard of a career called 'actuaries', and that is primarily who is tasked with: researching, analyzing, and helping develop premiums to match the risk that they are studying.

Jungle Tip #1. Myth- Get over "It's not gonna happen to me." This part of the book is to get us to open our eyes and turn away from the NIMBY mindset. You know NIMBY? Not in my back yard. It's a near cousin of "It's not gonna happen to me." Well, research shows otherwise.

This info is taken directly from the Council for Disability Awareness, which is a non-profit organization dedicated to educating the American public about the risk and consequences of experiencing an income-interrupting illness or injury. So this isn't some insurance company (or agent) trying to scare you here. This is a non-profit group dedicated to helping educate people. And really, that's one of the overarching principles that we operate from in our agency as well as this book: **to help better educate you so that you and your family can make good decisions to help prepare, protect, and recover from life's unexpected events.**

Disability happens more often than you'd imagine:

- Just over one in four of today's 20 year olds will become disabled before they retire.[1]
- Over 37 million Americans are classified as disabled—about 12% of the total population. More than 50% of those disabled Americans are in their working years, from 18-64.[2]
- 8.8 million disabled wage earners, over 5% U.S. workers, were receiving Social Security Disability (SSDI) benefits at the end of 2012.[3]

- In December of 2012, there were over 2.5 million disabled workers in their 20s, 30s, and 40s receiving SSDI benefits.[20]

Chances of being disabled:

The following statistics come from CDA's PDQ disability risk calculator:[4]

- A typical female, age 35, 5'4", 125 pounds, non-smoker, who works mostly an office job with some outdoor physical responsibilities, and who leads a healthy lifestyle, has the following risks:
    » A 24% chance of becoming disabled for 3 months or longer during her working career;
        - with a 38% chance that the disability would last 5 years or longer,
        - the average disability for someone like her lasting 82 months.
    » If this same person used tobacco and weighed 160 pounds, the risk would increase to a 41% chance of becoming disabled for 3 months or longer.
- A typical male, age 35, 5'10", 170 pounds, non-smoker, who works an office job with some outdoor physical responsibilities, and who leads a healthy lifestyle, has the following risks:
    » A 21% chance of becoming disabled for 3 months or longer during his working career;
        - with a 38% chance that the disability would last 5 years or longer,
        - the average disability for someone like him lasting 82 months.
    » If this same person used tobacco and weighed 210 pounds, the risk would increase to a 45% chance of becoming disabled for 3 months or longer.

---

20 http://www.disabilitycanhappen.org/chances_disability/

Here is a sample of factors that <u>increase</u> the risk of disability: excess body weight, tobacco use, high-risk activities or behaviors, chronic conditions such as diabetes, high blood pressure, back pain, anxiety, or depression; frequent alcohol consumption; and substance abuse.

A sample of factors that <u>decrease</u> the risk of disability: maintaining a healthy body weight, no tobacco use, healthy diet and sleep habits, regular exercise, moderate to no alcohol consumption, avoidance of high-risk behaviors including substance abuse, maintaining a healthy stress level, and effective treatment of chronic health conditions.[21]

So we know that disability can happen the question is, what to do about it? Well, before we even discuss the insurance aspects, I want to highlight the OTHER factors that you can do to help lessen your chance of disability. First off, notice above how being overweight almost doubled your statistical chances of being disabled.

How to lower your odds of becoming disabled

An ounce of prevention, the old saying goes, is worth a pound of cure. That's certainly true about disability. You can immediately reduce your odds of becoming disabled by making a few commonsense improvements in the way you live.

- **Embrace a healthy lifestyle**
  Oh, you've heard this one before? It's still true. Shedding bad habits and adopting healthier ones creates an abundance of benefits--not just for you, but for the people who love you and want you to stick around a long time.
- **Quit smoking**
  It's no secret that nicotine use has been linked to a variety of life-threatening illnesses, from cancer to heart disease and stroke. If you're a smoker, make quitting your top priority. Need help kicking the habit? The American Cancer Society can help.
- **Get regular checkups**
  Think of your doctor as an ally who helps *keep you well*, not just

---

21   http://www.disabilitycanhappen.org/chances_disability/disability_stats.asp

the person who *treats* you when you're sick. Regular checkups and screenings are vital, especially if you or your family are predisposed to certain medical conditions. Wondering about which screenings and immunizations you need? Ask your primary healthcare provider or visit the US Department of Health and Human Services website.

- **Get regular cancer screenings**
  Early detection saves thousands of lives every month. Family history and certain risk factors sometimes indicate that a person's screenings should start at a younger age. Ask your doctor or visit the American Cancer Society website for more information.

- **Watch your weight**
  those extra pounds can cause big trouble. They strain your heart, raise your blood pressure, and significantly increase your risk of a heart attack. Eat more high-fiber, nutrient-rich fruits and vegetables and fewer high-fat foods. For more dietary information, visit the US Department of Agriculture's Choose My Plate Website. Calculate your body mass index (BMI), to assess your personal situation with this tool from the National Heart Lung and Blood Institute.

- **Get regular exercise**
  A healthy life requires periodic physical activity. To prevent heart disease, cancer, high blood pressure, and obesity, the American Heart Association recommends 30-60 minutes of exercise at least four times a week.

- **Avoid excessive drinking**
  While drinking in moderation is usually fine, heavy drinking can lead to liver damage and other serious health risks. The Substance Abuse and Mental Health Services Administration can answer your alcohol questions.

- **Become safety-minded**
  Disability-causing incidents can spring up when you least expect them. Stay alert for possible dangers. Drive defensively. Wear your seatbelts. At work or play, always use the

recommended safety equipment. For more information, visit the National Safety Council.
- **"Watch your back."**
Back injuries and arthritis are the leading causes of disability. You can reduce your chances of injury by losing weight, doing gentle stretching exercises before a rigorous workout, and sound weightlifting techniques. The Cleveland Clinic Health Information Center is an excellent source of information.
- **Cultivate your mental and emotional health, too**
Good relationships and a positive mental attitude really help. Maintain contacts with family and friends. Stay active and involved through work, recreation, and perhaps volunteer work in your community. Yes, it's a 24/7 world, but no one can work 24 hours a day. Take time for relaxation and doing things that make you happy. Reducing stress reduces the likelihood of some physical illnesses. For more information, visit Mental Health America.[22]

Jungle Tip #2- Basics of disability insurance.

First off, there are 2 types of disability insurance; short term and long term disability. Short-term disability is meant to come into play very quickly after injury or illness (sometimes starting as quickly as a few days after the claim has taken place) and cover a percentage of weekly salary paid out (typically between 50% to 70% of weekly salary).

The duration of short-term disability benefits is typically between 10 to 26 weeks. By the very definition, short-term disability is just that, limited in nature.

Long-term disability has many of the same features but willing to cover you for a longer period of time, such as 3 or 5 years or until you are age 65. Here are the key terms to know:

Monthly benefit- The amount of money the insurance company will pay you on a monthly basis. This is usually based on your after-tax income, and the insurance company will replace up to 60% of

---

[22] http://www.disabilitycanhappen.org/reducing_chances/

after-tax income. The **reason for this is that disability payments are not taxed (under most circumstances; there are some instances where it is taxed) so you are getting approximately the same amount of your usual monthly income**.

For example, let's say you make 50k a year. That is about 4k/month pre-tax, but assuming a 25% tax bracket, you are really getting $3000 per month a normal monthly basis. The concept with disability income is that if you take 60% of the 50k that's about 30k per year, WITHOUT taxes being removed from your paycheck. It is important to note that when you are on claim your disability income payments are not taxed by the IRS, SO long as YOU make the payments for the disability income yourself. IF your employer makes the disability income payments, then the income can generally be taxed. [23] As always we do not give tax advice so please consult with your tax advisor or CPA for details on your personal situation.

Benefit period. The biggest part of the disability income insurance, outside of the monthly benefit amount, is the benefit period. The benefit period states how long the policy will last. Common terms are 3 years, 5 years, or until age 65. As with all insurance the longer the term or benefit period the more expensive the policy premium will be. The shorter the benefit period, the less the premium will be.

Elimination period. This is a fancy way of saying how long until the insurance company starts paying your claim. (IE. This is your deductible). Common elimination periods can be 60, 90, or even 180 days. The longer the elimination period, the less expensive the policy. The shorter the elimination period the more expensive the premium will be. For planning purposes you would want to make sure you have a minimum of your elimination period's worth of savings to bridge the gap until your benefits kick. For example, if I pick a 90 day elimination period you would want to make sure you have at least 90 days worth of savings that you can live off of to maintain your quality of life until

---

[23] https://www.irs.gov/Help-and-Resources/Tools-and-FAQs/FAQs-for-Individuals/Frequently-Asked-Tax-Questions-and-Answers/Interest,-Dividends,-Other-Types-of-Income/Life-Insurance-and-Disability-Insurance-Proceeds/Life-Insurance-and-Disability-Insurance-Proceeds-I

your payments kick in. Ideally, **most financial planning experts will recommend an emergency fund of 6 months worth of savings.**

Occupation definition. Own occupation vs. Any occupation. This is big, especially for specialists (IE. Surgeons, Dentists, Doctors etc). **Ideally you want a policy definition that says "own occupation,"** meaning that if you can't do YOUR own occupation, your benefits would trigger. This is different than any occupation. For example, in the case of a surgeon, he may become disabled to the point that he could no longer do surgery; however, could he perform ANY job at all? Perhaps he could now teach medicine at a college?

According to disability attorney John Tucker, "...once that changes to Any Occupation, that means you are being evaluated based on your ability to do any job. Often, Any Occupation definitions do not have an equivalent earnings requirement either; so if you can be a ticket taker at a movie theater making minimum wage, your claim would be denied under that type of definition."[24]

So in terms of a policy definition, look for policies that have a structure saying your benefits would kick in for your "own occupation."

Jungle Tip #3. Understand how the application process works. With disability income insurance, there are a few things to be aware of in terms of the application process. First, they will ask for financial evidence to substantiate your income. Likely, an insurance company will want to see tax returns and pay stubs for the last 2 to 3 years to make sure you really are earning what you say you are earning. As you can imagine, someone may say they make 100k per year, yet in reality, it may be nowhere near that and the insurance company would be on the hook for more than what they should be. Insurance fraud is a huge issue and costs the industry and consumers millions of dollars; so this is one of the reasons you will be asked to prove your income. Second, there will be a medical evaluation. This will include the application, a Paramed exam

---

[24] http://erisadisabilitylawyer.com/2012/07/18/own-occupation-vs-any-occupation-definitions-of-disability/

(which is where a nurse will do a mini physical), a medical records review, and possibly other exams as deemed necessary, like an EKG/ECG test on your heart. The important thing to know is that once **you get your disability income insurance policy, it CANNOT be cancelled or taken away from you based on future health issues.** That's why you have it right? So do it now, while you're healthy and young!

In summary, **"oatmeal is better than no meal,"** and without the ability to earn money due to disability, injury, or illness, life can become extremely challenging. Look to maximize your benefits through a group plan if available at work, and also protect yourself with a standalone **long**-term disability policy outside of work should you lose your job, start a business, or move.

6

Life Insurance - A love letter to your family

VERY FEW TOPICS evoke as much fear as talking about dying. While most people say public speaking is their greatest fear, the reality is if you want to really kill the mood in a room the next time you are at a cocktail party, bring up the subject of setting up your will, or planning your funeral, or taking out life insurance. We don't want to think about it, do we? I had a client one time tell me, "Every day above ground is a good day," and I believe that to be so true.

Yet as I tell my team regularly at Strategic Insurance, no one wakes up and says, "Today's the day I'm going to get into a car accident. Or, today is the day my home will be broken into and burglarized." And we sure aren't waking up saying, "today is the last day I will spend on this earth." That being said, we all personally know people who have died young, so why do we think it could never happen to us? That's probably the subject of a whole other book, but I want to share the first time this hit me, this idea of dying young. It was the year after I graduated college, in 2003. At the time, I was brand new in the financial planning and insurance business, and I got my alumni magazine from Gettysburg College. I remember reading of a classmate of mine who was killed in a car accident. While I didn't know Keith well, I sure remember him. He was a football player, tall and strong, who was in some of my management classes. He was a nice, quiet guy. One day, this 21-year old man, freshly graduated from college, woke up and then the next day he was gone from this earth. Tragic.

The reality is that we deal in a world that is full of challenges and troubles that are unpredictable and can be harder than we could ever imagine at times. That's part of life on earth, and that's not going to change anytime soon.

Jungle Tip #1. Don't be like the other 95 million Americans. According to recent industry studies, approximately 95 million Americans have no life insurance at all, and only 1/3 of Americans have individual policies outside of work (more on this later.)[25]

So not to belabor the point about the reality that 100% of people who are born die and that it can happen to anyone, let's look at what type of coverage options are out there:

Term Insurance- pure cost of the insurance. Think of it like renting. Quite simply, this is the least expensive option (in the short term) to cover you and your family. People often think life insurance is much more expensive than it is, and in fact, term life insurance is one of the few policies that have come DOWN in premium over the last decade (as people are living longer so the companies can charge lower rates for a longer period of time). Term lengths come typically in 10, 20, and 30 year options. The longer the term, the more expensive the premium.

You probably have seen an ad on the TV or heard an ad on the radio for term insurance that goes something like this, "A healthy, 40-year-old male, can now get $500,000 of 20 year term insurance for $38/month." Not bad for a little over $1/day. **Skip Starbucks twice a week and you can budget for life insurance protection for your family.**

The advantage of term insurance is that the rates stay level for every year the policy is in force. So 19 years from now, when EVERYTHING

---

[25] http://www.foxbusiness.com/personal-finance/2014/01/22/life-insurance-myths-shouldnt-believe/

will be more expensive due to inflation, you would still pay $38/month for your 500k in term life insurance coverage.

I recommend term insurance to our clients often to cover their biggest needs; mortgage, college planning, income replacement etc. This is especially critical during the years where the need is the greatest, which are typically a husband & wife raising a family with children. The only downside to term insurance is what happens AFTER 20 years if I still need life insurance? After 20 years the policy will renew but at a much higher rate.

Permanent insurance. Think of it like owning a home. This is a permanent policy with other benefits. When I say permanent insurance, there are multiple forms of this type of insurance including whole life, universal life, and variable universal life. I don't want to get too bogged down in all of the intricacies of each type of insurance, but I will give a big-picture overview of each, so if you have questions please feel free to email me Info@GetStrategicIns.com or call our office at 727-213-1890 for a deeper discussion on the types of permanent life insurance.

Overall permanent life insurance policies (in any form) last longer than term insurance. As stated above, what happens if you need coverage past 20 years? What if you didn't pay off all the debt you thought you would or you had kids later in life and still have the need for life insurance? Those inexpensive term rates you got 20 years ago are likely going to be 4 to 6 times what they were originally. We contrast this with a permanent policy that would go all the way to age 100 (or beyond), meaning your rates are in essence locked in forever. So right there is a benefit of permanent insurance, in that you are much more likely to see some beneficiary (i.e. who the policy benefit will go to after you die) get paid on the life insurance.

Whole Life Insurance- This is probably the oldest form of permanent life insurance and also the most expensive. Benefits include not just locked in rates for life but also cash value accumulation and dividend growth. If price is not an issue, this can be a great option in certain circumstances. That being said, these policies were pushed heavily from the 1940s to the 1980s and often times are not truly the best product fit for families.

Universal Life Insurance- This is a policy that has a death benefit (i.e., how much the insurance company pays out) and cash value (an account that accumulates cash based on guaranteed and current interest rates). The difference between this and whole life is that you have some flexibility in terms of how much you pay each month, whereas with whole life you do not. For example, you may have a $100,000 universal life insurance policy and you have to pay a minimum of $50 per month but could put more into the policy. I call this my "Gumby policy," in that it is flexible. This policy also has a cash value component. The cash value is going to be tied to interest rates. The higher the interest rates are, the better the policy will perform in both cash value and how long it will last. And that is the caution with universal life insurance and the tradeoff for that flexibility. Because there is flexibility, there is also a danger in not properly understanding the functions of the policy. This happened a lot in the 1980s when interest rates were very high with the federal funds rate—as high as 20% at one point! So you would see a universal life insurance policy with certain projections of both the cash value and how long the death benefit would last (which is also based in part on the interest rates at the time) on say 17%, and yet here we are 30 years later, and interest rates are virtually 0%. So the takeaway **here is that you need to understand how interest rates can affect these policies,** and it's always important to do periodic reviews with your insurance agent or advisor.

Variable Universal Life- This adds yet another dimension in terms of options. These policies have both death benefit and cash value accounts, yet the underlying cash value account can be tied to a combination of stocks, bonds, and mutual funds for potentially higher growth, yet also more risk. Whereas regular universal life insurance is tied only to a fixed income like interest rate, the cash value in VUL (variable universal life) is tied to the stock market. You also can have a range of payments subject to a minimum to continue to fund the policy.

No Lapse Guarantee Universal Life Insurance. This policy is a UL policy with no cash value but a guaranteed option for the death benefit. Think of this like a "guaranteed permanent term insurance." You don't have some of the bells and whistles in terms of cash accumulation, yet you do have the best option to lock in your rates long term for your death benefit.

Jungle Tip #2- How to determine the amount of coverage you should have. Much like asking a roomful of attorneys for their opinion on a case, there are lots of ways to look at how much coverage you should get. Here are a few routes:

- **Look at 8 to 10 times annual income. This is a rough and ready rule of thumb for how much coverage to pick to cover your family.**
- Do a life-needs analysis. There are several calculators online; and here is a good 3rd-party calculator from www.lifehappens.org [26]
- Work backwards based on your budget. In my 10 plus years of insurance and helping families with their finances, I've been in appointments where I basically do a pen and paper version of the life-needs analysis. We look at loans and debt, education planning, and income replacement. Sometimes the true need can be a big number. While I am passionate about what we do and have seen the impact of life insurance firsthand on a family who lost their father or mother **I'm also aware that we are all on a budget.** So how much can you budget for this valuable protection? $50/month, $100/month, or more? Then you can work backwards and determine how much coverage we can get you based on what you are willing to budget. I often say, "Oatmeal is better than no meal," so whatever you can secure is better than nothing.

Jungle Tip #3- Consider the impact of inflation on the purchasing power of the life insurance policy amount you pick. Financial experts often call inflation the silent killer as it erodes your purchasing power over time. Think about the example grandkids heard from their grandparents; "When I as a kid milk and eggs were a nickel!" Now, you can spend $4 to $6 easily on milk and eggs at the grocery store. Most everything goes up over time in terms of its pricing. SO your 500k life

---

[26] http://www.lifehappens.org/insurance-overview/life-insurance/calculate-your-needs/.

insurance policy today, IF it was paid out 15 years from now, the policy would have the purchasing power of $350,000 in today's dollars. The reality is **for MOST people with a house, a few cars, and two or three kids need at least $500,000 to $1,000,000 especially when factoring inflation over time.**

Real Life Impact: One of the most startling days in my career was getting news that a client I had previously written term life insurance for was murdered on an interstate in Florida due to a case of road rage. He was 36. He had three kids and ran a successful painting business. We had written a 400k 10 year term policy, and his wife, who was still in shock and deeply distraught, was grateful he had done planning. Her only comment was that she wished he had more. We all know people who have passed away too young, and we have all seen families who have had loved ones leave this earth too soon, leaving the family in a precarious financial position. As I sit here and write this, my nine-month-old daughter Abigail Grace is learning to stand and likes to climb up on my legs as they hang over the couch. Its moments like this that make remember how precious her life is and what a great honor it is to be her father and protect her. I can›t help but think of the responsibility I have as her father to make sure that regardless of what happens to me, she will have the same opportunities I have had and even better. Mark Twain famously quoted, "Life insurance is that love letter," so make sure you have yours in order.

With term rates being very inexpensive, most healthy 40- to 50-year-old males and females can get 500k of 10-term life insurance for less than $50/month. If you are interested and want a proposal on life insurance or a review of your current protection, you can visit my special website at http://protectmywhy.com and fill in your information. Abbie and Asher are part of my "whys" that I want to protect, I'm sure you have plenty in your circle, and this life insurance is the key to making sure your "whys" are protected should something happen to you.

7

Flood Insurance- Splish, splash, I'm taking a bath

FIRST OFF, LET me say that where I live in Clearwater, FL, it seems that EVERYONE lives in "the highest part of the county." Now, I live in Florida, and it is flat as a pancake, no mountains around, and we are surrounded by water on each side. We have more risk of hurricanes each year than any other state in the country. That being said, I can't help but chuckle a little bit when I hear "I live in the highest part of the county." The reality is that **since 1978, FEMA has paid out almost 48 BILLION in flood damage across the US.** The risk is huge, and approximately 25% of all flooding occurs in "preferred" flood zones.[27]

What does this mean? Basically, **we all face the risk of flooding.** Think about it. Not a year goes by where we don't see catastrophic flood damage in various parts of the US, from the Midwest to the northeast and western parts of the US. There are two groups of flood insurance: preferred flood and required flood. Preferred flood means you live in a B, C, or X flood zone and are at a lower risk of flooding. Note, as stated above, that you still have a 25% chance of having a

---

27 https://www.floodsmart.gov/floodsmart/pages/flood_facts.jsp

flood, so just because you are in the preferred flood zone does NOT mean you can't or won't experience a flood. The risk is just less. The second group is what I'm calling a required flood zone. These tend to be flood zone A, V, or VE. When you are in one of these flood zones and have a mortgage on your house, the bank will REQUIRE you to have flood insurance—no two ways about it.

First, let's be clear and define what exactly a flood is. According to FEMA, who regulates flood insurance, a flood is:

- A general and temporary condition of partial or complete inundation of **2 or more acres of normally dry land area or of 2 or more properties (at least 1 of which is the policyholder's property) from:**
    - » Overflow of inland or tidal waters; or
    - » Unusual and rapid accumulation or runoff of surface waters from any source; or
    - » Mudflow;

The really important note here is that it must apply to two or more properties or acres. So if we have really bad rain, and JUST your house floods, this will not trigger your flood insurance.[28]

I also want to clarify something here that we get asked frequently. The question I get goes like this, "What if a pipe breaks and causes a flood in my house?" Good question, and your homeowner's policy DOES cover this under "sudden and accidental water damage" on most policies. As always, it's important to check with your agent and your specific policy to verify coverage.

Jungle Tip #1- Protect your home against flooding with a preferred risk flood insurance policy. My question to you is, assuming your home is your biggest asset, is it worth approximately $1 a day to protect it against catastrophic loss of flooding? The average cost of a preferred risk flood insurance policy as of 2015, covering $250,000 of building coverage and $100,000 of contents coverage is $430/year. That works out to $1.13/day, to have coverage for your home. Again, skip that Starbucks once or twice a week and you have saved enough

---

28 https://www.fema.gov/national-flood-insurance-program/definitions#F

to buy flood insurance. Note that this rate is true ACROSS the country, as long as you are in a B, C, or X flood zone, which are the preferred flood zones. One other recent option that has come up in the last few years is private market flood. Private market flood is NOT underwritten by the Federal government and as such can set their prices however they wish. Again keep in mind for so long because flood was regulated and subsidized the private market stayed away from flood insurance as they were not able to compete with the Federal government. However, in recent years as the government has increased flood rates, in certain areas private markets (such as Lloyds of London or AIG) have been able to compete and beat the federal government rates. For us, it's one more "tool in the tool belt" to ensure you are getting the best coverage and rates possible. As always, check with your local insurance agent or email me at Info@GetStrategicIns.com for more info.

Jungle Tip #2- If you are in a flood zone, review your deductible for savings. While preferred risk policies are optional, IF you are in flood zone A, AE, V or VE and have a mortgage the bank will REQUIRE you to have flood insurance. So the bank requires you to have it; the question is, what can I do to help get the best rate possible? Flood insurance is also unique in that **the rate is the exact same with ANY company authorized to write flood insurance**, as FEMA (Federal Emergency Management Agency sets the rates, and administers set the money for claims. The insurance companies really just handle the processing of policy issuance, administration, and claims. So the rate will be the same, but there are a few things you can do to help the premium. As always, the higher your deductible, the lower your premium. This is a predominant theme in this book, (along with finding a good local independent agent): by increasing your deductible you can lower your premium.

Jungle Tip #3- Review your contents coverage and understand how it is paid in a claim. The other thing you can do, in addition to increasing your deductible, is to review your contents coverage and determine the proper amount of coverage for you and your family. Now this is an area that can vary WIDELY. Some people spend hundreds of thousands of dollars on their furniture alone. While I find that more the outlier than the norm, if you have a lot of contents coverage, make sure you take up to the $100,000 maximum and potentially an excess policy (more on that later). However, many families have less than $100,000 in contents. The other thing that is super important to **note is that contents are always valued at actual cash value in flood insurance.**

How flood insurance contents policies are valued:

Actual cash value (ACV) is the value at the time of loss, less the value of its Physical depreciation. **Personal property is always valued at ACV.** [29]

So what does this mean in laymen's terms? **Actual cash value is basically the VALUE your item has today.** Here's an example I use with clients all the time. Let's say you have living room furniture and a TV that is seven years old. The value of those items today (e.g., think about you selling it on EBay) may be a total of $700 for three pieces of furniture and a TV; it may be less, depending on the condition the item is in. Now let's say you need to go out and buy those items NEW. It may cost you $2,000 or more, and that is what the replacement cost value is: the cost of buying it new today. With flood insurance contents, you always get that depreciated value; so you may not need as much coverage depending on the age and condition of your contents.

In summary, for pennies on the dollar, do yourself a favor and get some flood insurance!

The flood insurance marketplace has changed and now there are several private market flood insurance options available. Jungle Tip #4 for flood insurance is to ask your agent IF there is a private market flood option that would be more competitive than the national flood insurance program options? We have seen instances where the private market flood option is thousands of dollars less than the national flood insurance option. You will be glad you did especially if you live in a high-risk flood area. Of course you can email us at Info@GetStrategicIns.com to review your flood insurance to see what private market options may be available.

29

8

Long-term Care Insurance - Age with the dignity you deserve

NO ONE WANTS to get old, except those under the age of 18. Some of the best advice I ever heard was, "Don't get old." Yet we know it is inevitable. We age, and we breakdown or wear out. But there is good news, and that is that we are all living longer. According to the online database Our World in Data at the time of America's independence, the average life expectancy was not much past the age of 35.[30] Now, according to the World Bank, a female born today has a life expectancy over the age of 80 in several countries, including America.[31]

So far, this is probably no big news flash or earth shattering information. Something that you probably don't think about is the consequence of living longer. For instance, in the early 1800s a man or woman who had a heart attack or stroke was sure to die. Today, those same conditions, even for those in advanced age, may not kill,

---

30 (http://www.ourworldindata.org/data/population-growth-vital-statistics/life-expectancy/),
31 (http://data.worldbank.org/indicator/SP.DYN.LE00.FE.IN/countries).

thanks to advancements in medicine and ground-breaking technology. As a result of us living longer, but "wearing out slowly," our care needs are greater. What do I mean by "care needs?" Think about what you do on a daily basis that you take for granted. You get up, eat, shower, walk, run, play, talk, drive etc. For some people, those activities are huge struggle to do each day because of their health challenges....and they may not be improving. What we are talking about here is what the insurance industry calls "Activities of Daily Living" or ADL's (our industry loves acronyms!) **ADL's include things such as eating, toileting (using the restroom), and transferring (moving about as you need).** These are a few of the main activities that an insurance company looks at with regards to opening up a long term care claim. So if you have medical condition (IE. Alzheimer's) and your doctor writes that you will have trouble with 3 activities of daily living for a prolonged period of time (usually 6 months or more) that would trigger the policy.

With long-term care insurance, **you have a choice in how your care plays out as you advance in years and deal with the challenges of aging**. Yes I realize this is as much fun as a root canal—I really do. Even as I sit here writing this, as my fingers are flying, my mouth puckers, and my skin crawls just thinking about some of this. Regardless of how I feel that, it doesn't change the truth of the reality.

Jungle Tip #1- Understand the basics- Daily benefit amount and where the policy will cover you. Like any insurance product, LTC (which is the acronym I will use for this coverage) is about cost and benefits. So how does the policy work you ask? Well, the first thing to consider is how big of a "bucket" of benefits you want, which starts with a daily benefit amount. In essence, the daily benefit amount is the coverage that the insurance company will pay daily for your care. This could be anywhere from $100 per day to $500 per day or higher. So say you broke a hip and need care 3 days a week for the next year. If your daily amount was $300 that means on a monthly basis the policy would pay out $3600 ($300 per day x 3 days per week x 4 weeks in a month). Most long term care policies are designed to cover you first for home health care (which means bringing help into your home like nursing aides and assistants), assisted living and then a nursing home if need be. Again the big thing here is independence and choice of care which suits you and your family's needs.

Jungle Tip #2- Pick your time frame for coverage to last. Today you will see benefit coverage periods of 3 years, 5 years, and 10 years. In the past, insurance companies offered lifetime benefit periods, but this is a rare occurrence today based on the claims the insurance companies have seen in the last handful of years. The longer the coverage period, the longer the policy will last, and the bigger your "bucket" of benefits will be.

Jungle tip #3- Look to add the inflation guard rider to your policy. In many ways, inflation is the "silent economic killer" to our finances. We all know $100 today is NOT what $100 was 10 or 15 years ago because of inflation (i.e., the relatively incremental rise in prices of products and services over a period of time which devalues our purchasing power.) An inflation guard will ensure that when you select a $200/day benefit, 10 or 15 years from now you will have the equivalent purchasing power of $200 at that time WHEN you need it.

Jungle Tip #4- Calculating the cost of care. It is important to understand what your future costs for care could be. Today we can ask Google just about anything, and a search of long-term care costs will yield several results. For Florida, according to the Florida Health Care Association, the median cost of a private room in an Assisted Living Facility is $36,000/year. The average annual cost for a semi-private room in a Nursing Home is $87,000/year.[32]

The costs for home health care aides can vary widely based on the nature and extent of care needed, but rates can range from $15 to $22/hour. So check with your state resources to identify your approximate care costs.

From there, it's a matter of analyzing your assets to determine, if there is any portion you want to self-insure, and then work on your estimated needs and you can they better choose your benefits. For example, let's say you want to create a plan that has $350,000 of coverage. You could choose a plan with a $200/day benefit for 5 years.

---

32 http://www.fhca.org/media_center/long_term_health_care_facts

So let's say that you need help in your home just 3 days per week to do chores, housework, help with errands, and go to doctor appointments; the policy would respond by paying out $600/week, or $2,400 for the month.

Jungle Tip #5- When to buy.... Sooner than you think. While different financial experts and analysts will provide you with different recommendations, one thing we know for sure is this: Like most insurance, **the older you get, the more it is going to cost you**. Many financial experts will recommend buying long-term care insurance between 55 to 60 years of age. While that is true, in doing research, I came across an interesting article from Bankrate.com, which asked, "Given an example of 45, 55, and 65, which option would be the most cost effective in terms of purchasing an LTC policy?" **To my own surprise, it was 45. Even though the 45 year old would pay for a longer period of time, the difference in price that the 10 or 20 years makes was tremendous.**

"A married couple at age 45, for example, would now each pay $2,444 annually for a policy with a $200-per-day benefit ($6,000 per month) that kicks in right away for home care and after 90 days at a facility from an insurance company. By age 80, each person would have paid $85,540, according to Cornerstone's math.

If the couple chose to take the $2,444 and invest it at 5 percent, they would have $14,180 saved by the time they turn 50 in 2016, Cornerstone calculated.

However, if at 50 they chose to buy a similar policy as the one they opted not to get five years earlier, the annual premium would be $3,797 each, and the net cost at age 80 would increase to $99,722, including applying the $14,180 in invested funds.

At 55, the annual premium would rise to $5,579 each, and the net cost at 80 would total $107,189, including applying $32,277 in invested funds, Cornerstone found.

By 60, the premium would zoom up to $8,197 each, and the net cost at 80 would be $108,563, offset by $55,375 in invested funds.[33]

---

[33] http://www.bankrate.com/finance/insurance/best-age-to-buy-long-term-care-insurance-1.aspx#ixzz3QWdaY5AG

In conclusion, according to the US Department of Health and Human Services, **approximately 70% of people age 65 and older will need long-term care**.[34] That is a staggering statistic that is hard to ignore meaning 7 out of 10 people will need this protection **OR wind up self-insuring and paying ALL of the costs out of their hard earned assets.** The question is, what are you doing to prepare yourself, your spouse, and your children for your care? For the baby boomers, long-term care insurance is what life insurance was to the "greatest generation" and following. That is a critical part of their family's financial plan to ensure their stability. A necessity is to plan well for the future of your family. To get more information or specific pricing, email Info@GetStrategicIns.com and put "long term care" in the subject, and one of our team members will be in touch.

---

34   http://longtermcare.gov/the-basics/who-needs-care/.

9

Accident Insurance and what else DON'T I need?

SO, YOU MAY be thinking, "Ok insurance guy, you probably want me to buy any and every product out there, right?" Not so fast "Joe consumer," I routinely tell clients when doing reviews **that certain insurance is not worth it in my opinion.** The reality is, ALL insurance comes down to risk management. We EACH have to weigh out the risks and potential benefits of the insurance we are purchasing. Some of this is made easy for us in that it is REQUIRED, and thus our goal should be to maximize our value, which we define as the combination of the best coverage and pricing available. Auto and home insurance are examples of this. If you want a driver's license and valid registration, you need proof of auto insurance. Does this mean you should buy the cheapest possible liability coverage? Obviously not because you would be putting your assets and family at risk if you were underinsured and at fault in an accident. Does this mean you need to carry 1M of liability with a 5M umbrella if you are a 30-year-old married couple? Of course not, as this would be ridiculously over-insuring a young couple just starting out with no justification of the assets warranted to require so much insurance. Now, what if I am a retired doctor with a net worth of 15M dollars? Certainly, a 5M umbrella seems prudent for asset protection and is not a case of overkill.

What's my point? Each and every person has to make the best decision for their family. That being said, there **here are a few types of insurance that just don't plain make a lot of sense to me.**

Jungle Tip #1- Ditch the accidental life insurance. Why do I say this? Statistically speaking, your chances of dying in some sort of accident (car, plane, falling down, etc.) are 41 per 100,000 deaths in 2013. That means your statistical **odds of dying in an accident is 0.0041% or less than half of half of half of 1%.**[35] The chances are very, very slim. Some accidental life insurance policies are SUPER inexpensive, and when I come across them and read through the contract, it is almost invariably because the policy is an accidental death policy only. Whatever the cost is, it's not worth it, as you are better off having a regular life insurance policy that doesn't have such extreme exclusions to it.

Jungle Tip #2- Ditch the dental insurance. A lot of people want and ask about dental insurance in our agency. For the most part, dental insurance is expensive for its benefits, especially on individual policies. The typical person or family is going to spend between $30 to $50/month for a policy that likely will give them a maximum of $1000 to $1500 annual benefit. So really, you are paying $400 to $600/year for a $1000 to $1500 benefit, most of which you aren't likely to use beyond a few cleanings and X rays. Instead, I recommend www.dentalplans.com, which offers plans from $79 PER YEAR for individuals, to $130/year for families. These plans give you anywhere from 10% to 60% off any of your dental services without limits. For most families, this will be a better route both financially and in terms of benefits. Now what about group dental insurance? I would encourage you to find out how much is coming out of your paycheck and what kinds of benefits you are getting with it. Every plan and policy can be different, so it's

---

35 http://www.cdc.gov/nchs/fastats/accidental-injury.htm.

important for you to investigate for yourself. My point is that unless you have severely bad teeth and know you have many expenses coming, **often times the dental insurance is overpriced and under used.**

Jungle Tip #3- Want an extra $250,000 at retirement? Ditch the low deductibles. If you don't learn anything from this book other than this, you will walk away with a tactic to save you thousands and thousands of dollars over a lifetime just by increasing your deductibles. **With all insurance, the lower the deductible, the higher the premium, and the higher the deductible, the lower the premium.** The days of $250, $500, and even $1000 deductibles are gone in my opinion. Take your deductibles up. Home, auto, flood, and health insurance are all areas you can take your deductible up higher and save money. Let's just say here, as an example, that previously you had a $250 deductible for your comp and collision on your auto insurance. This is what insures your vehicle. By going from $250 to $1000, let's say you save $300/year. Now let's assume on your home insurance you have a $1000 deductible. By going to a $2500 deductible per year, you save another $400/year. On your health insurance, you go from a $2,500 deductible to a $5,000 deductible and save $600/year. If you also live in a flood zone and have a $1,000 deductible for flood insurance on your building and contents and you go to a $3,000 deductible, you're saving another $350/year. By making these changes, we were able to carve out $1650/year in savings. Now let's assume you made this change at age 35 and invested that $1650 in a ROTH IRA that earned 7% annually.

>Initial Investment: $1,650 Interest Rate: 7%
>Regular Investment: $1,650/year
>Years Compounded: 35
>**After 35 years, you will have:**
>$261,673.57[36]
>Initial Investment $1,650.00
>Regular Investment $57,750.00
>Interest $202,273.57

***Note this is purely a hypothetical example and not any guarantee of actual investment results.

---

36 Compound Interest Calculator http://www.interestcalc.org/

That is a powerful illustration and one that exists in lots of insurance portfolios across America.

In summary, there are certain things you probably DON'T want and/or need when it comes to insurance. **Dental insurance, accidental life insurance and low deductibles are 3 that come to mind.** That being said, every case and client situation is different, and as always, you need to do what is best for your situation and family. If you have any questions on these concepts or want to review policies that you may be wondering if you really need or not, go ahead and email me at Info@GetStrategicIns.com with a copy of the policy, and in the subject, write, "Do I need this insurance?"

10

Umbrella Insurance - Protect against the big one

FUNNY...AS I SIT here at my house getting ready to right about umbrella insurance, it is pouring rain out. It's one of those days where God just opens up the spigots, and it is coming down by the bucket full. Now, if you were sitting where I am right now, there is NO way you would go outside without an umbrella over your head. It doesn't make sense. You would get beyond drenched—to that soaking point which is just no fun.

Well many like you wouldn't leave the house without an umbrella on a rainy day; I wouldn't leave your driveway or home without an umbrella insurance policy. So what exactly is this umbrella coverage? Simply put, **an umbrella policy provides 1M or more of additional liability coverage above your underlying assets, such as your car or house.** It can also cover additional real estate holdings (whether they be rentals or vacation homes), boats, and recreational vehicles.

Why you need it? Just like a real umbrella goes over your head to protect against the wet weather, an insurance umbrella goes over your head to protect against catastrophic lawsuits.

Jungle Tip #1- Umbrellas are one of the most inexpensive, cost effective ways to protect your ass(ets). I'm having a little fun on a serious subject, but the truth is that umbrella policies can help cover your butt big time, for pennies on the dollar. For $1,000,000 of umbrella coverage, the typical family would pay between $250 to $400 per year to cover their primary home and a few cars.

Jungle Tip #2- Statistics show that personal injury lawsuits are on the rise.

According to the latest major research from the National Center for State Courts, as well as the Legal and Finance Journal: "According to the National Center for Health Statistics, over 31 million injuries occur to people throughout the U.S. each year that necessitate a doctor's care, almost two million people sustain injuries that require some degree of hospitalization, and 162,000 people die from their injuries. The National Highway Traffic Safety Administration reports that over three million injuries and 40,000 deaths occur just from the 5.5 million car accidents in the U.S. annually, with another 60,000 personal injuries and 5,000 deaths resulting each year from truck accidents. **Personal injury lawsuits might occur due to a traffic accident, a dog bite, a construction accident, medical malpractice, or a defective product. Unfortunately, these incidents are all too commonplace in American society.**"[37]

Bottom line is, chances are that your biggest risk of a lawsuit is in a car accident; so this alone should be reason for the umbrella protection. Add in a home with a pool and kids and/or a rental property, and you quickly see the exposure and need to protect yourself.

Jungle Tip #3- A word from financial guru, Dave Ramsey: Buy an umbrella when your net worth is 500k or more.

Dave Ramsey, one of America's authoritative leaders on personal finance, recommends getting an umbrella when your net worth is 500k or more. Remember, net worth is what you own minus what you owe. Dave says, in a Fox Business article, "I would **get umbrella insurance, which is extra liability insurance, when you reach the half-million mark in net worth.**"[38]

---

37 http://legalfinancejournal.com/personal-injury-lawsuits-in-the-u-s-a-brief-look/ and http://www.ncsc.org/Services-and-Experts/Areas-of-expertise/Civil-justice/Civil-Justice-Survey/Civil-Justice-Survey-Data.aspx

38 http://www.foxbusiness.com/personal-finance/2013/11/05/when-do-need-umbrella-insurance/

A closing word from the real world. My 2nd year in the insurance business, at a previous company, we had a client who was coming home from church and killed a man on a motorcycle. Very tragic. We had recommended to the client many times to increase their liability limits and take out a liability umbrella. This couple owned a business and made good money, which was reason enough for the additional protection. I'm sure the emotional impact upon BOTH families was tremendous. Both the family of the man who was killed on the motorcycle AND the impact on the woman and her family who was guilty of driving the vehicle that took that man's life. As bad as the emotional impact is, the real world there was a significant financial impact. Our whole mission and goal is "to make sure that the families and businesses we work with are Prepared, Protected and able to Recover from life's unexpected events." The small premium for the umbrella insurance protection is well worth the peace of mind it buys to know your family would be protected.

Summary

Pulling it altogether

INSURANCE IS A fact of life. You may not like it, but it is necessary to protect your assets in today's complicated world. So in order to maximize your value, which we define as the best coverage at the best rate possible, remember these parting pieces of advice:

Jungle Summary Tip #1- ALWAYS look at higher deductibles. This one piece of advice alone could save you thousands of dollars per year, and I would argue tens of thousands of dollars over the next few decades. Remember, the higher the deductible, the lower the premium, and the lower deductible, the higher the premium.

Jungle Summary Tip #2- Shop around for alternative companies annually. Depending on where you live, the insurance market place may be volatile. Here in Florida, we have faced issues with hurricanes, sinkholes, and auto insurance fraud in the last 10 years alone. If you had chosen a home and auto insurance company 10 years ago and made no changes, you likely would have paid way more than you should have. The day of being with the same company for 40 years, (like State Farm and All State) has likely passed.

Jungle Tip #3- Find a good independent insurance agent. Go to www.trustedchoice.com to find an agent in your area. In today's environment, I believe that having a pro-active agent who understands the state insurance environment and has systems in place to ensure you're getting the best value is more important than a single company.

Insurance is something you never want until you absolutely need it. Then it's like water or oxygen. If your house burned down or you got sued for $1,000,000 in a tragic at-fault car accident. All of a sudden you will cling to your insurance like a parachute on a plane that is going down. Hopefully this book has given you some practical, tangible tools to make sure you get the best value and survive the insurance jungle!

www.ingramcontent.com/pod-product-compliance
Lightning Source LLC
Chambersburg PA
CBHW021003180526
45163CB00005B/1874